THE SHRIKE

By JOSEPH KRAMM

 Random House, New York

THE SHRIKE

PUBLISHED IN NEW YORK BY RANDOM HOUSE, INC., AND
SIMULTANEOUSLY IN TORONTO, CANADA, BY
RANDOM HOUSE OF CANADA, LIMITED
LIBRARY OF CONGRESS CATALOG CARD NUMBER: 52-7497

Photographs by Alfredo Valente

PRINTED IN THE UNITED STATES
AT THE COUNTRY LIFE PRESS, GARDEN CITY, N.Y.

TO THE MEMORY OF
MY MOTHER AND FATHER

The Shrike was first presented by Jose Ferrer at the Cort Theatre, New York City, on Tuesday, January 15, 1952, with the following cast:

(In Order of Appearance)

MISS CARDELL	*Phyllis Hill*
FLEMING	*Tom Reynolds*
MISS HANSEN	*Jennette Dowling*
DR. KRAMER	*Stephen Elliott*
PERKINS	*James Hawthorne Bey*
GROSBERG	*William Bush*
DR. BARROW	*Isabel Bonner*
PATIENT	*Vincent Donahue*
ANN DOWNS	*Judith Evelyn*
JIM DOWNS	*Jose Ferrer*
DR. SCHLESINGER	*Somer Alberg*
DON GREGORY	*Philip Huston*
SAM TAGER	*Will Lee*
GEORGE O'BRIEN	*Martin Newman*
JOE MAJOR	*Joe Comadore*
JOHN ANKORITIS	*Will Kuluva*
FRANK CARLISLE	*Leigh Whipper*
WILLIAM SCHLOSS	*Billy M. Greene*
DR. BELLMAN	*Kendall Clark*
MISS WINGATE	*Mary Bell*
HARRY DOWNS	*Edward Platt*
TOM BLAIR	*Arthur Jarrett*

Produced and directed by Jose Ferrer
Associate Producer Milton Baron
Setting and lighting by Howard Bay
Costumes by Edith Lutyens

SCENES

ACT ONE

Scene   I—11:30 in the morning—Tuesday.
Scene II—2:00 A.M.—the next morning—Wednesday.
Scene III—Noon—two days later—Friday.
Scene IV—11:00 A.M.—three days later—Monday.
Scene V—Afternoon—immediately following.

ACT TWO

Scene   I—Just before lunch—the next day—Tuesday.
Scene II—2:00 P.M.—the next day—Wednesday.
Scene III—Close to 9:00 P.M.—the same day.
Scene IV—2:00 P.M.—the next day—Thursday.
Scene V—3:00 P.M.—five days later—Tuesday.

ACT THREE

Scene   I—1:30 P.M.—two days later—Thursday.
Scene II—Afternoon—four days later—Monday.
Scene III—2:00 P.M.—three days later—Thursday.
Scene IV—10:00 A.M.—the next day—Friday.

ALL THE ACTION TAKES PLACE IN CITY HOSPITAL

ACT ONE

ACT ONE

Scene I

Ward MN 3—City Hospital.

We see part of the ward, three or four beds. No ornamentation in the room, no flowers. Only metal cabinets for the patients' belongings next to each bed.

The windows differ from other sections of the hospital in that there are heavy wire screens in front of the windows themselves, which means that the windows can only be opened or closed with cranks inserted into sockets for that purpose.

Downstage is the corridor. On the left, near the door, there are two desks and two chairs. Desk lamps, papers, patients' charts and telephones are on the desks.

At the left end of the corridor is a door. This is the only door to this ward, to this floor, as a matter of fact, from any other part of the building—and it is constantly locked. Nurses, attendants and doctors use their keys to get in or out.

TIME: 11:30 in the morning—Tuesday.

There are patients in the three or four beds that we see. One is asleep, one reading, one staring into space, one talking to the student nurse, MISS CARDELL, *at his bedside.*

The nurse in charge, MISS HANSEN, *a middle-aged woman who has been soured rather than mellowed by her contact*

3

with illness, is seated at the first desk, the one closest to the entrance to the ward. She is making notes on some of the charts.

DR. KRAMER, *a tall, good-looking man, in his late thirties, is standing near the other desk, reading a chart.*

MISS CARDELL

You were smoking, Mr. Fleming.

FLEMING

(*A man of about fifty*)

No, I wasn't.

MISS CARDELL

A man with a heart condition like yours—honestly! Give me the cigarettes, Mr. Fleming.

FLEMING

I haven't got any cigarettes.

MISS CARDELL

(*Lifts the blankets*)

I don't have all day—now give me the . . .

FLEMING

Look in the cabinet, if you don't believe me.

MISS CARDELL

Do you want me to call an attendant, Mr. Fleming? (*He subsides*) Then let me have the cigarettes.

FLEMING
(*Pulls the blanket back—irritably*)
All right. (*Reaches under mattress at head of bed*) Here.

MISS CARDELL
I'll have to report it—you know that. Where are the matches?

(*Phone rings at* MISS HANSEN's *desk.*)

MISS HANSEN
MN3—Miss Hansen.

FLEMING
Here.

(*Takes matches from pocket of his pajamas.*)

MISS CARDELL
Where did you get them?

MISS HANSEN
Right away. (*She hangs up*) Emergency suicide coming up, Dr. Kramer.

DR. KRAMER
(*Without looking up*)
Is there a bed?

MISS HANSEN
Miss Cardell, is there a vacant bed?

MISS CARDELL

Not in this ward. Mr. Fleming has been smoking, Miss Hansen.

MISS HANSEN

(*Paying no attention*)

Hm-hmmm.

DR. KRAMER

And call Dr. Barrow, Miss Hansen.

MISS HANSEN

Yes, Dr. Kramer. (*On phone*) Dr. Barrow, please. Dr. Kramer, MN 3. Emergency suicide. (GROSBERG *appears, pushing empty wheel chair.* MISS HANSEN *sees him*) Oh, Mr. Grosberg, will you and Mr. Perkins bring a bed to 3? Emergency.

GROSBERG

(*Shrugs his shoulders. He is effeminate*)

I don't know where we'll find one unless somebody dies.

(*Turns wheel chair around and goes off.*)

MISS CARDELL

(*Still with* FLEMING)

That doesn't make any difference. You know the kind of patients we have here. Suppose one of them took those matches while you were asleep and set fire to something?

FLEMING

You're right. I'm sorry.

6

MISS CARDELL
(*As she goes*)
I should think for your own good . . . Honestly!

(*She exits.*)

MISS HANSEN
(*Hangs up phone; to* DR. KRAMER)
Dr. Barrow will be up as soon as she can.

DR. KRAMER
Thank you.

(PERKINS *and* GROSBERG *enter, wheel in a bed in time to hear* MISS HANSEN'S *announcement to* DR. KRAMER.)

GROSBERG
Dr. Barrow's nice. You know her? She's a psychiatrist. You ever been psyched?

PERKINS
Uh—uh.

MISS HANSEN
(*Gets up from desk*)
Put it right here for now. We can move it later.

(*She indicates entrance to the ward, returns to the chair and sits down. The bed is wheeled into position.* GROSBERG *and* PERKINS *take folded linen from the bed.*)

7

GROSBERG
(*As they make the bed*)
I have a friend who's being psyched. He says it's wonderful. The things you say about yourself.

FLEMING
Hssst, Grosberg.

GROSBERG
He goes three times a week and he can't wait for the next session.

FLEMING
Hssst.

(GROSBERG *waves at him to be quiet.*)

GROSBERG
(*Going to* FLEMING)
Can't you see I'm busy? There's an emergency coming up—a suicide.

(FLEMING *gives him a dollar bill. As* GROSBERG *pockets the money he moves away again.*)

FLEMING
(*Whispers*)
Chesterfields.

GROSBERG
(*Finishes making the bed with* PERKINS)
Now what would a man want to do that for? Some woman,

8

I guess. It's always a woman. (*Bell rings*) There it is. We'd better hurry.

> (MISS HANSEN *starts for the door. She takes key from her pocket and opens door.*)

MISS HANSEN

The suicide?

ATTENDANT

Yeah. Here's his card.

MISS HANSEN

This way. (ATTENDANT *wheels in the patient on a high carriage, then leaves.* MRS. DOWNS *starts to follow.* PERKINS *moves the carriage*) Who are you?

ANN

His wife.

MISS HANSEN

This way.

> (DR. KRAMER, *meanwhile, rises, takes the sphygmomanometer from his desk, and goes to carriage. He ties the rubber pipe on the patient's arm and takes his blood pressure.* ANN *stands close by.* DR. BARROW *enters and goes directly to the bed.*)

DR. KRAMER
(*When he has finished, he looks at* DR. BARROW)
110 over 60. (*Slaps the patient's face several times*) Wake up! Wake up! (*Looks to* ANN) What's his name?

ANN

Jim.

DR. KRAMER
(*Slapping his face hard*)
Jim! Wake up, Jim! (*A low grunt from* JIM) That's it!
Wake up!

DR. BARROW
What did you take?

(JIM *grunts again.*)

ANN
Phenobarbital.

DR. KRAMER
Let *him* answer.

ANN
I'm sorry.

DR. KRAMER
(*Shaking* JIM)
What did you take?

JIM
(*Thickly, through a haze*)
Phen o bar bital.

DR. BARROW
What?

DR. KRAMER

Speak up, Jim! Again! What did you take?

JIM

(*No clearer than before*)

Phen o bar bital.

DR. KRAMER

When? (*No answer—slaps him again*) Come on, Jim! Wake up! When did you take it? (*No answer*) How many did you take?

JIM

(*Slowly, thickly*)

A hun dred and fif ty six.

DR. KRAMER

What?

(*He looks at* DR. BARROW.)

DR. BARROW

That's impossible.

DR. KRAMER

You ask him again.

DR. BARROW

Jim! Wake up, Jim! (*She shakes him*) How many pills did you take?

11

JIM

A hun dred and fif ty six.

DR. BARROW
(*Her hand on his face*)

He's so cold.

ANN

He was lying on the floor. It was an unheated apartment.

DR. BARROW

That may have saved him. If the place had been warm, it would be all over.

DR. KRAMER

When did he take them—that's more important!

DR. BARROW

Jim! Try to tell me, Jim! When did you take the pills?

(*There is no answer.*)

DR. KRAMER
(*Calmly—to* PERKINS *and* GROSBERG)

Move him to the bed. Miss Hansen, order a saline solution with high vitamin content for intravenous injection. Perkins, screen the bed. Grosberg, get a stomach pump.

(PERKINS *gets screen.* GROSBERG *goes for stomach pump.* MISS HANSEN *goes to her desk. The screen is placed around the bed by* PERKINS, *who exits.*)

12

(*To* ANN)
We can't tell yet. He'll be on the critical list for a while. You can stay here if you like.

(*Goes to desk with* ANN. *She sits*)
Miss Hansen, I want special nurses for at least forty-eight hours.

MISS HANSEN
I'm not sure we can get them. This is Thanksgiving week—most of them will be away.

DR. KRAMER
We must have them.

MISS HANSEN
What about her? Can she afford special nurses?

ANN
I'll manage. Please get them. Get anything that's needed.

(MISS HANSEN *picks up phone to call—her voice in ad lib undertone.*)

DR. KRAMER
(*Pause*)
Now, how did this happen?

ANN
I don't really know. I got a phone call from his brother at about 9:30 this morning. . . .

13

DR. KRAMER
(*Puzzled*)

Wait a minute—weren't you there? I thought you were his wife.

ANN

I am. We were separated. He was living in this cold-water flat.

DR. KRAMER

I see.

ANN

His brother's a businessman in a small town near Pittsburgh. When he called me—it's a funny thing, I couldn't sleep all night. I knew something had happened to Jim—his brother said he had just received a letter from Jim saying he was going to take the pills. He told me to get over there as quickly as possible, and of course I did. (*Fighting her tears*) I called the police—(*The tears give way*) I'm sorry—Doctor—I'm not an hysterical woman.

DR. KRAMER

That's all right. You've been fine.

ANN

I called the police and told them what happened. (MISS CARDELL *and* PERKINS *enter with saline solution and sterilizing pan*) I gave them the address and thank God they were there by the time I arrived. They tried to break the door, but the lock held, and one of them went up to the roof, came down the fire escape and climbed in through the window. He let us in. My husband was lying on the floor in the living room.

(PERKINS *leaves.*)

14

DR. KRAMER

What did the police do?

ANN

They shook him and slapped him, the way you did—and they asked him what he took.

DR. KRAMER

Was he able to tell them?

ANN

Yes. He said phenobarbital, the way he told you.

DR. KRAMER

This happened about an hour ago, I take it.

ANN

When we found him?

DR. KRAMER

Yes.

ANN

Just about.

DR. KRAMER

We've *got* to find out when he took the pills. Do you have any idea at all, Mrs. . . .

ANN

Downs. Well, let me see—this is Tuesday, Tuesday. I talked with him on the phone about 12:30 Sunday night.

(MISS CARDELL *exits.*)

15

DR. KRAMER

And not since?

ANN

No. We made an appointment to see each other at four
o'clock Monday afternoon—that was yesterday—at my place.
He didn't show up. That's the last I knew until his brother
called me this morning.

DR. KRAMER
(*Writing on the chart*)

Well—we'll see. . . .

ANN

Oh—the eh—the postmark on the letter.

DR. KRAMER

What letter?

ANN

The one he sent . . .

DR. BARROW
(*Comes from behind screen to* KRAMER's *desk—
addresses* ANN)

Excuse me—are you Charlotte?

DR. KRAMER
(*To* DR. BARROW)

This is his wife. (*To* ANN) Dr. Barrow's a psychiatrist.

DR. BARROW

What's your name?

16

ANN

Ann.

DR. BARROW

I wanted to identify the name Charlotte.

ANN

She's just someone he knew.

DR. BARROW

I see.

(*She looks at* ANN *briefly and returns to* JIM.)

DR. KRAMER

You were speaking about a postmark on a letter.

ANN

Yes—the one he sent to his brother. There'd be a New York postmark on it—you might be able to tell approximately from that. I can call him on the phone.

MISS HANSEN

What is his religion, Mrs. Downs?

ANN

Protestant.

MISS HANSEN

Any special sect?

ANN

He wasn't a regular churchgoer—Why?

17

MISS HANSEN

He'll have to be given last rites. I'll call the minister.

(*She turns back and picks up phone.*)

ANN

(*To* DR. KRAMER—*again fighting for control*)
It's as bad as that?

DR. KRAMER

It's just a precaution. I'd call his brother, if I were you,
Mrs. Downs.

ANN

But . . .

DR. KRAMER

It's all right. Why don't you call him now? The phone is
downstairs.

ANN

I want to be here when . . .

DR. KRAMER

You have no idea how many men have walked out of here
after last rites have been said over them.

ANN

You're sure it's all right?

DR. KRAMER

Yes. Make your call. Everything is being done for him that
can possibly be done.

18

ANN

Thank you, Doctor. May I see him—for just a moment?

DR. KRAMER

All right.

(ANN *goes behind the screen. A brief pause.*)

ANN
(*Quietly*)

Jim! Jim!

(*After a moment, she appears and goes to the door.* DR. KRAMER *unlocks it, lets her out and locks it.*)

(*The lights fade quickly.*)

ACT ONE

Scene II

The same.

About 2:00 A.M.—the next morning—Wednesday.

The ward is dark. Light comes from desk lamps and the dim light in the corridor.

ANN *is sitting in the doctor's chair. She is trying hard to keep awake.* MISS CARDELL *comes from* JIM's *bed with a thermometer in her hand. She goes to her desk and records the temperature.*

MISS CARDELL

You ought to go home, Mrs. Downs.

ANN

I'd rather stay, if it's all right. At least *here* I know what's happening.

MISS CARDELL

But it's nearly two A.M. You ought to get some rest.

ANN

I'm all right. If only I could get a cup of coffee.

MISS CARDELL

You'll find some in the kitchen—down the hall. (ANN *starts to get up*) Never mind—I'll get it for you.

21

ANN

Thank you.

MISS CARDELL

You've been wonderful, I'll say that for you. (*As she goes for the coffee*) Also, you're crazy—no man is worth it.

DR. BARROW

(*Enters. To* MISS CARDELL *as she meets her*)
Mrs. Downs still here?

(MISS CARDELL *nods to the desk and leaves.*)

DR. BARROW

How do you feel? (ANN *nods*) You've been a big help, but you must have some reserve.

(*Checks* JIM's *pulse. Goes to foot of bed, looks at chart.*)

ANN

How does it look, Dr. Barrow?

DR. BARROW

It's more on the good side, I think I can say. You've been with him all day?

ANN

I haven't left him for a moment.

DR. BARROW

Has he spoken yet?

ANN

A few things.

DR. BARROW

What?

ANN

Why didn't you let me die, he said—why didn't you let me die. He repeated it several times. I wanted to question him, but I didn't think I should.

DR. BARROW

Oh, by all means—that's most important. When he starts talking again, you must try to keep him awake.

ANN

I'm afraid to do something wrong.

DR. BARROW

Not at all. You must question him, talk to him—get all the information you can. The things he says now are the most important. That's what he really thinks and feels. As he regains consciousness, he will begin to build the walls again. You understand?

ANN

Hm-hmm.

DR. BARROW

Cigarette?

ANN

No, thank you.

DR. BARROW

Self-deception. His defenses will come back to protect him.

(*Lights cigarette.*)

ANN

I understand.

DR. BARROW

You spoke to his brother this morning?

ANN

Yes.

DR. BARROW

Was there anything in the letter—any reason for taking his life?

ANN

I don't think so. His brother read the letter to me on the phone. I don't remember anything.

DR. BARROW

Have you any idea why Jim didn't leave a letter for *you*, Mrs. Downs?

ANN

No—unless he felt . . . I don't know. (MISS CARDELL *enters with coffee*) Oh, thank you, Miss Cardell, you're very kind.

MISS CARDELL

Not at all.

24

DR. BARROW

Coffee! I'd love some. (*A questioning look at* MISS CARDELL) Would it be too much trouble?

MISS CARDELL
(*Doesn't like to run errands for doctors*)
Not at all.

(*Exits.*)

DR. BARROW

What does your husband do, Mrs. Downs?

ANN

He's in the theatre.

DR. BARROW

Singing—dancing?

ANN

No—it's what they call the legitimate theatre—he's a director.

DR. BARROW

Has he worked recently?

ANN

No. Several years ago he directed a show that got good notices. . . .

DR. BARROW

On Broadway?

ANN

Yes. The critics said he was a fine, new talent.

DR. BARROW

Then I don't understand. . . .

ANN

Well, that's the theatre. It ended right there. He expected
to be flooded with offers from other producers, the movies,
what not—but nothing came of it. Time went by—several
years now, in fact—the show was forgotten. He never got
another job.

DR. BARROW

I see. Well, that's only part of the reason. Is there anything more?

ANN

He had to start all over again—anything at all, just to
make a living. It made him very unhappy. (JIM *moans*)
That's Jim—he's trying to move. Oh, yes, once he said—why
did they tie my hands and feet?

DR. BARROW

You understand—we *had* to tie him—the intravenous
needle in his arm. (*Another moan*) Maybe he's awake. (*They
go to* JIM's *bed.* BARROW *turns on bed lamp*) What's the
matter, Jim?

JIM

(*Still indistinct—in everything he says there is a sense
of struggle*)
Why don't you let me die?

26

DR. BARROW

Why do you want to die, Jim?

JIM
(*Loudly*)

I'm no good. No good!

FLEMING
(*Sits up in bed*)

What the hell is he yelling about?

DR. BARROW

Quiet, Mr. Fleming.

FLEMING
(*Lies down again*)

Christ—try to sleep . . .

ANN

He *is* very loud.

DR. BARROW

He's fighting. (*She leans over the bed*) Jim, why do you
say you're no good?

JIM

Nowhere, after all these years . . .

ANN

There's still time, dear. You'll be all right.

JIM

I had my chance—I didn't make it. . . .

ANN

You will. . . .

JIM

There's no time any more. I'm an old man.

ANN

You're not, Jim. I told you so many times. . . .

DR. BARROW
(*To* ANN, *quietly*)

How old is he?

ANN

Forty-two.

DR. BARROW

But that's young.

ANN

I know, but he's had that idea for several years. He insists he's an old man.

DR. BARROW

Why do you think you're an old man, Jim?

JIM

Why?

DR. BARROW

Yes, why do you think you're an old man?

JIM

Why don't you let me die? I'll only have to do it again.

ANN

No, dear, things will be different. . . .

DR. BARROW

You're a young man, Jim. There's time to change.

JIM

Don't tell me that. . . . (*Suddenly yells*) Why am I tied?

ANN
(*Quietly*)

Jim?

JIM

What?

ANN

I love you. I love you. Do you hear me, Jim?

JIM

It's too late, Ann. I don't want you to love me. (*Then, more subdued*) A hundred and fifty-six pills . . .

DR. BARROW

Of course, *that* I can hardly believe.

ANN

He's said it several times.

(ANN *goes to the desk.*)

DR. BARROW

I know.

JIM

The taste of those pills.

DR. BARROW

Jim, how do you know there were 156 pills? (*No answer*)
Jim! Jim! (*She turns off the lamp*) That's a strange detail
to remember—the number of those pills. It's so exact.

ANN

I don't understand it myself, Doctor.

DR. BARROW

Are you in the theatre, too, Mrs. Downs?

ANN

I was. I was doing very well in the theatre when I met Jim.
When we married I felt one career in the family was enough,
so I gave it up.

DR. BARROW

Did Jim realize what that meant for you?

ANN

I think so.

DR. BARROW

Do you regret it?

ANN

(*A brief pause—a bitter smile*)
We all have our vanity, Doctor.

DR. BARROW

Of course. Do you have any children?

ANN

No.

DR. BARROW

How long have you been married?

ANN

Nine years. (*Suddenly, she bursts into tears*) I love him,
Dr. Barrow. I know he loves me.

DR. BARROW

That's good. That will help.

(*The lights fade quickly*)

ACT ONE

Scene III

The same.

About noon—two days later—Friday.

A bright sun makes the ward look almost cheerful. GROS-
BERG *is serving "dinner"—trays of mush known technically
as a "soft diet."*

JIM DOWNS *is sitting up in bed. From his attitude, there
is no awareness that anything at all unusual has taken place.
Now that he's alive, the only thing that matters is to get out
of the hospital as soon as possible. There is a strange combina-
tion of adult intelligence, good humor, and, at times, almost
childish naïveté.*

*GROSBERG enters, pushing a serving wagon on which are
trays of food.*

FLEMING
(*As* GROSBERG *leaves tray*)
What's for lunch? S.O.S.?

GROSBERG
(*In agreement*)
S.O.S.

JIM
(*Tentatively*)
Mr. Grosberg?

33

GROSBERG

What?

JIM

May I speak to you a moment?

GROSBERG

What do you want?

JIM

Would you do something for me?

GROSBERG

What?

JIM

(*Takes note from under his pillow—looks at* GROSBERG)
Would you see that this gets mailed?

GROSBERG

Your wife'll be here, won't she? Why don't you ask her?

JIM

Well—I—I'd rather you did it. I—would you mind?

GROSBERG

(*Looks at* JIM)
That's worth a pack of cigarettes, at least.

JIM

I haven't got anything just now—but—I'd appreciate it.

THE SHRIKE

GROSBERG
(*His hand out*)
Gi' me.

JIM
Thanks a million.

(*The bell at the door rings once.*)

GROSBERG
(*Puts letter in his pocket as he goes to the door*)
Where'd you get the paper and pencil?

JIM
(*An embarrassed smile*)
I borrowed it.

GROSBERG
From Mr. Fleming?

FLEMING
There's no law against it, is there?

GROSBERG
(*As he opens the door*)
Did I say anything?

(*He admits* ANN. *She goes to* JIM.)

FLEMING
Hi, Mrs. Downs.

ANN
(*Smiling*)
How are you, Mr. Fleming?

FLEMING
First rate, Mrs. Downs.

ANN
(*At* JIM's *bed*)
How do you feel, Jim?

JIM
Fine.

GROSBERG
(*Returns to bed and feeds the man who is staring into space*)
You going to feed your husband again, Mrs. Downs?

JIM
I don't need anybody to feed me.

GROSBERG
(*Feeds the silent one, slowly. To* JIM)
You're a big boy now, huh? You weren't so big the last couple of days. Your wife did everything for you.

JIM
(*Looking at* ANN)
She did? (ANN *smiles at* JIM) Thanks, Ann.

36

ANN

Eat your dinner. And then I have some wonderful news for you.

JIM

What?

ANN

Eat your dinner first.

JIM

Oh, Ann—that's not fair. What's the news?

ANN

The Joe Williams office called you.

JIM

What—for a job?

ANN

That's what they said. They want to see you.

JIM

When?

ANN

Monday afternoon. Naturally I didn't tell them what happened.

JIM

Of course. Monday. That's wonderful. Ann, I ought to try to get up—I ought to try to *walk*.

ANN

(*Laughs gently*)

Really, Jim—yesterday at this time you weren't able to sit up.

JIM

Will you let me try?

ANN

Please, Jim, don't. You're not strong enough.

JIM

(*Trying to get up*)

I know I can get up, Ann.

ANN

Eat your dinner first.

JIM

Let me stand for a minute, and then I'll eat.

ANN

Jim, if the doctors thought you could get up, they'd let you.

JIM

Then let me talk to one of them. Is there a Dr. Barrow? I seem to remember that name. And a Dr. Kramer—is that right?

ANN

Yes. Dr. Kramer is your physician. He pulled you through.

JIM

If I could only talk to one of them. I feel much better now, Ann. Don't I *look* better to you?

(DR. BARROW *enters.*)

ANN

Much better.

JIM

Well?

ANN

Dr. Barrow! Jim was just wanting to speak to you.

JIM
(*As* DR. BARROW *comes to his bed*)
Are you Dr. Barrow? You're very attractive.

DR. BARROW
(*Smiles*)
What do you want?

JIM

I want to get up. I want to start walking around. I have an appointment on Monday. I'd like to keep it.

DR. BARROW

Is it important?

JIM

It's for a job. That doesn't happen every day.

DR. BARROW

Isn't it more important that you get well?

JIM
(*His look is pleading*)
It's the closest I've been to a job in God knows how long.

DR. BARROW
With whom do you have this appointment?

JIM
With Mr. Williams. He's a producer.

DR. BARROW
We can tell him you're ill.

JIM
Please don't tell him that. I'll be fine by Monday.

DR. BARROW
Well, I can't say. I'm not your medical doctor. I'm the psychiatrist. Dr. Kramer will have to pass on you physically.

JIM
May I see Dr. Kramer?

DR. BARROW
He doesn't have the final say, either. Dr. Schlesinger—the chief psychiatrist on this floor—is the boss.

JIM
(*Hopefully*)
When will I see him?

DR. BARROW

When Dr. Kramer says you're well. But I'll use whatever influence I can. When is the appointment?

JIM

On Monday.

DR. BARROW

I'll try. I'll call Dr. Schlesinger now.

(*She starts out.*)

JIM
(*As* DR. BARROW *goes*)

Thank you, Doctor.

ANN

Now eat your dinner, Jim.

JIM

I'll drink my coffee. What do they call this stuff, anyway?

ANN

It's like baby food. They call it a soft diet. If you want to get up, you'd better eat—you'll need the strength.

JIM

Just one spoonful, that's all.

(*Tastes food, grimaces.*)

41

ANN

(*Laughs*)

It's wonderful to see you in such good spirits again. When you come home, I'll make everything you like.

JIM

(*Stops, suddenly fearful*)

Ann, I'm not going to come home.

ANN

You can't go back to that cold-water flat. It's too depressing.

JIM

(*Urgently, but hushed*)

Ann, you're making a mistake. . . .

ANN

We don't have to discuss it now, Jim.

JIM

I don't want to hurt you again, but you're taking it for granted I'll go back with you. . . .

ANN

It's all right, Jim.

(DR. KRAMER *lets himself in with his key. He locks the door from the inside.*)

JIM

It's *not* all right, Ann. I'm not ungrateful—but things are different.

ANN
(*Silences* JIM *with her hand*)

Here's Dr. Kramer.

DR. KRAMER

Good morning, Mrs. Downs. (*Comes to the bed, to* JIM)
How do you feel?

JIM

Fine. My wife has been telling me wonderful things about
you, Dr. Kramer. I guess I owe my life to you.

DR. KRAMER

I'm glad to hear you're grateful. You weren't for a while.

JIM

Doctor, I have a very important appointment on Monday.
Do you think I'll be able to keep it?

DR. KRAMER

When did *this* happen?

JIM

Just now. Ann took the call. I feel much better. Don't you
think I can make it?

DR. KRAMER
(*Thinking about it*)

Today's Friday—from the medical point of view it's quite
likely you can leave by Monday. You've come along pretty
well with your wife's help. You ought to be very grateful.

43

JIM

Yes, I know.

DR. KRAMER

When I saw how well she was taking care of you I dismissed the special nurses.

JIM

Really? That's wonderful, Ann. Will you let me get up, Doctor? I'll show you I can do it.

(DR. BARROW *and* DR. SCHLESINGER *enter.* DR. BARROW *stops for a moment.* DR. SCHLESINGER *continues to desk.*)

DR. BARROW

Mrs. Downs. (ANN *turns*) May we see you for a moment?

ANN

Of course.

(ANN *goes into corridor to meet* SCHLESINGER.)

DR. BARROW

Dr. Kramer? (*He turns to her*) Please.

(DR. BARROW *and* DR. KRAMER *join the others in the corridor.*)

FLEMING
(*To* JIM)

The star chamber is in session.

(GROSBERG *takes trays and exits with cart.*)

DR. SCHLESINGER

(*Having picked up chart from desk, he turns to* ANN)
Mrs. Downs?

ANN

Yes.

DR. SCHLESINGER

I'm Dr. Schlesinger.

ANN

How do you do?

DR. SCHLESINGER

Won't you sit? (*She does*) Have you any way of knowing whether this is a legitimate appointment or not?

ANN

Oh, yes. He has the appointment. The call came to me.

DR. SCHLESINGER

I see. What do you think, Dr. Kramer?

DR. KRAMER

Medically, I think it's possible.

DR. SCHLESINGER

Dr. Barrow?

DR. BARROW

Well, he said several times, in the unconscious state, he was a failure. Maybe if he got this job, it would be a healthy thing for him psychologically.

DR. SCHLESINGER
(*Thumbing the chart*)

Hm-hmm—perhaps it can be managed. (*Almost as an afterthought*) Mrs. Downs, what do you think?

45

ANN

Of course, I'd like to see Jim get the job, but do you think it's possible?

DR. SCHLESINGER

Why not?

ANN

Well, you would know more about these things than I. . . .

DR. SCHLESINGER

What's troubling you, Mrs. Downs?

ANN

Well, his eyes . . . They don't always seem to focus. . . .
(*The doctors look at each other.*)

DR. BARROW

He sounds rational most of the time, doesn't he?

ANN

Yes, it's only once in a while he'll say something wild and incoherent.

DR. SCHLESINGER

Like what?

ANN

I don't remember at the moment. Doctor, what would happen if he kept the appointment and didn't get the job?

DR. SCHLESINGER

Of course, it would be another failure and that would be worse.

DR. BARROW

Yes, that's true. But, somehow, if it's important . . .

DR. SCHLESINGER

And I see the chart indicates he said many times he would do it again.

DR. KRAMER

Isn't that a normal reaction? I mean, it isn't at all unusual for a man to say such a thing unconsciously, so soon after making the attempt.

DR. SCHLESINGER

Yes, I know, but . . .

DR. KRAMER
(*To* DR. BARROW)

He hasn't said it since the first day, has he?

DR. BARROW

No.

ANN
(*Reluctantly*)

No.

DR. SCHLESINGER

It would still be a great risk.

DR. KRAMER

We have until Monday.

DR. BARROW

Suppose we see what happens. Dr. Kramer, you see what *you* can do about Mr. Downs, and we'll take it from there.

DR. SCHLESINGER
(*Looks briefly at* DR. KRAMER. *Takes the charts*)

I'll have a talk with him on Monday. (*To* ANN) I'd like to speak to you first, if possible, Mrs. Downs. Can you be in my office at eleven on Monday?

ANN

Certainly.

DR. SCHLESINGER

Good. (*He and* DR. BARROW *start to leave*) Oh, one more thing, Mrs. Downs. (*He returns to* ANN) I've been getting several phone calls a day from a Charlotte—somebody or other. She wants permission to see your husband.

(*A pause.*)

DR. BARROW

If this girl is an emotional complication for your husband . . .

ANN

I—I don't know what to say. The whole thing is so humiliating to me.

DR. SCHLESINGER

I must tell you, Mrs. Downs, as his wife, the law is entirely on your side.

(*Another pause.* ANN *finally looks to* DR. BARROW.)

48

ANN

I think it would be very bad for Jim to see her—don't you, Doctor?

DR. BARROW
(*To* DR. SCHLESINGER)

It would be a great strain.

DR. SCHLESINGER

I quite agree. I'll leave word downstairs she's not to be admitted at any time.

(DOCTORS SCHLESINGER *and* BARROW *go.*)

DR. KRAMER
(*To* ANN)

Come with me.

(*They go back to* JIM's *bed.*)

DR. KRAMER
(*With simulated enthusiasm*)

O.K., Jim. Let's see you go.

JIM
(*Sits up*)

What?

DR. KRAMER

Come on, get dressed. Get out of bed. You're as healthy as I am.

49

ANN
(*Startled*)
Are you serious, Dr. Kramer?

DR. KRAMER
(*With a wink to* ANN)
Of course I'm serious. Get him up.

JIM
Thank you, Doctor.

(*He moves slowly to put his feet on the floor.*)

ANN
(*All solicitude, she gets slippers from under the bed*)
Wait till I get these slippers on, dear.

FLEMING
(*Shouts*)
Oh, no! What are they trying to do to the guy? Kill him?

DR. KRAMER
Never mind, Mr. Fleming. Are you all right, Mr. Downs?

JIM
Fine—fine.

ANN
Hold on to me.

JIM
(*Holding* ANN's *arm*)
You see, I'm up.

(*He takes two or three steps.*)

FLEMING

Christ Almighty, he shouldn't be allowed—they're crazy. . .

JIM
(*His face beaming*)

I'm walking! I'm walking!

(*His legs give way and he starts to slump.*)

ANN
(*Calls*)

Dr. Kramer!

(DR. KRAMER *quickly goes to* ANN's *assistance, and helps her place* JIM *on the bed.*)

DR. KRAMER
(*Examines him*)

He's asleep. He'll be all right. He'll be fine by Monday. Worried, Mr. Fleming?

FLEMING

Those crazy bastards. I've never seen a hospital like this.

(*The lights fade quickly.*)

ACT ONE

Scene IV

The lights come up on DR. SCHLESINGER's *office—actually, just a table and two chairs in front of a hospital screen.*

11:00 A.M. *Three days later, Monday.*

DR. SCHLESINGER *is standing above the table.* ANN *is seated on the right.*

DR. SCHLESINGER

Has he ever had periods of depression before?

ANN

Certainly not to this extent.

DR. SCHLESINGER

Has he had psychiatric treatment before?

ANN

No. But I do think he needs help now.

DR. SCHLESINGER

Now tell me—has he spoken of doing this again?

ANN

Well, not in so many words, Doctor.

DR. SCHLESINGER

I see. Do you think we should keep him in the hospital for a while?

53

ANN

It would help Jim immensely, I think, to get over this
slowly. This is terribly important to me, Doctor. I feel he
needs time. If he could be in the hospital's care for a while,
I'm sure he'll realize our separation was a mistake.

DR. SCHLESINGER

That may very well be. The other day you were reluctant
to speak about Charlotte, Mrs. Downs.

ANN

Well, I can't help but feel that in some way she was responsible for this action.

DR. SCHLESINGER

Mrs. Downs, your husband will be here in a minute. I'd
rather he didn't see you. I want him to speak freely.

ANN

Of course.

DR. SCHLESINGER

Your having been with him so much is of enormous help
to us. I want to thank you, Mrs. Downs.

ANN

Not at all.

(*She gets up and starts toward right.*)

DR. SCHLESINGER

I'd suggest you leave *this* way. (*Indicates left*) You'll avoid
running into him.

ANN

Thank you.

DR. SCHLESINGER

You can wait in the next room.

(*She goes.* SCHLESINGER *sits at his desk.* JIM *enters right.*)

JIM

Dr. Schlesinger?

DR. SCHLESINGER

Come in, Mr. Downs. (*Pause*) Sit down.

JIM

Thank you.

(*Sits to right of desk.*)

DR. SCHLESINGER

How do you feel?

JIM

Fine.

DR. SCHLESINGER
(*Leans back*)

Well, I suppose you know you did a very serious thing. (JIM *shrugs and smiles*) You don't think it was serious?

JIM

I—I've always known that suicide was considered a crime against the state. I never understood why.

55

DR. SCHLESINGER

Is that all?

JIM

What else can I say? I did it—it didn't work—I'm alive now—thats all. I want to go home.

DR. SCHLESINGER
(*Without looking at* JIM)

Why did you do this thing, Mr. Downs?

JIM

Well, it's a complicated business. It wasn't just one thing. It was a lot of things. This was the week-end before Thanksgiving. I was having a friend to dinner—it was Saturday night—and I had spent practically my last cent—I was doing the cooking. When my friend arrived, she asked me what was for dessert. I didn't have any dessert. I couldn't afford it—and I started to cry.

DR. SCHLESINGER

Do you cry easily? I mean, at other times?

JIM

No, not often.

DR. SCHLESINGER

Well, not having dessert is hardly a reason to take your life.

JIM

I didn't mean to give that impression. It was simply an indication of how I stood. I had sixty cents left to last me eight days.

DR. SCHLESINGER
(*Always looking for the holes in a story*)
I understood you weren't working.

JIM
Not at my profession. I was teaching English privately and there was a check due in another week.

DR. SCHLESINGER
All right. Any other reasons?

JIM
A couple of years had passed since I did my last show. It didn't look as though I was ever going to get another one.

DR. SCHLESINGER
I understand you have an appointment for a job—this afternoon, as a matter of fact.

JIM
Yes. It could be an important break.

DR. SCHLESINGER
Hm-hmm—anything else?

JIM
I tried writing. Many years ago, while I was still in college, I was a newspaperman. And since I had the time, in the past few years, I mean—I thought I'd write. But nothing sold. I was working on a play, and I had finished the first act about a week before this happened. That Sunday night I re-read

what I'd written. I don't know what made me do it—but I did. And I thought the whole thing was terrible. Everything just seemed hopeless.

DR. SCHLESINGER

Why do you feel you're an old man?

JIM
(*Startled*)

When did I say that?

DR. SCHLESINGER

In the unconscious state.

JIM

Really? (*Pause*) Well, I guess I began to think about it when I was in the Army. I was too old to become an officer. I forced myself to try and keep up with the younger men. It wasn't easy. I was made painfully aware of the difference.

DR. SCHLESINGER

Were you overseas?

JIM

Yes—the whole European war—straight into Germany.

DR. SCHLESINGER

I see. And when you came out of the Army?

JIM

I found young men in the profession I didn't know. They didn't know me.

DR. SCHLESINGER

But age is no deterrent in your work, Mr. Downs. There are very old people still active in the theatre.

JIM

(*Irritated*)

Really, Doctor—I know that. But they aren't just starting out. I felt I was beginning all over again, and I thought I was too old for that.

DR. SCHLESINGER

I see. Are those all the reasons?

JIM

I'm sorry, Doctor. I know people have gone on against greater difficulties. Everyone reaches a low at some time in their lives. I just gave in to it, that's all.

DR. SCHLESINGER

But you said there were a lot of things. What about your wife?

JIM

Oh, yes, I remember. Sunday afternoon Ann called me. She said she wanted to talk to me, and we made a date for four o'clock the next afternoon—Monday.

DR. SCHLESINGER

And when did you take the pills?

JIM

Monday morning, at about 11:30.

59

DR. SCHLESINGER

Didn't you want to see your wife? (JIM *shrugs*) Was your relationship so bad you couldn't even talk to her?

JIM
(*Quickly*)

No. I saw my wife several times after we separated. It was just—well, on top of everything I knew she needed money. I thought of my G.I. Insurance Policy for ten thousand dollars. And I guess that clinched it. This was about twelve-thirty, that Sunday night. I wrote the first letter to my brother that night.

DR. SCHLESINGER

There was more than one letter?

JIM

I only mailed one. When I had finished writing the letter, it occurred to me that I hadn't paid the November premium on my policy, so I figured I'd have to wait until the next morning.

DR. SCHLESINGER

What for?

JIM

To check with the Veterans Administration to see if my policy was still in force.

DR. SCHLESINGER

Then what happened that night?

JIM
(*Naïvely*)

Nothing. I went to sleep.

DR. SCHLESINGER

Didn't you have any thoughts of death? Weren't you disturbed in any way?

JIM
(*Thinking about it*)

No. I slept like a baby. In the morning I got up, went out for the morning papers—had coffee. I remember reading about a director who had been signed for a new show, and thinking he didn't have any talent at all.

DR. SCHLESINGER

Yes. What happened next?

JIM

I phoned the Veterans Administration and found out the policy was in force for thirty-one days after the last payment So it was all right. I tore up the letter I wrote the night before, and I wrote another one, giving my brother the information on the insurance.

DR. SCHLESINGER

Did you give any reasons for taking your life?

JIM

No. Does a man ever really give reasons? (*There is a pause. The doctor says nothing*) I enclosed the key to my apartment in the letter, addressed the envelope, and sealed it.

Then—the only hesitation I had, was in when I should mail the letter—before or after taking the pills. You see, I didn't know what effect the pills would have, or how fast they would work. So I thought—if I mailed the letter first and then lost courage, or the will to do it, all I would succeed in accomplishing would be to scare the hell out of a lot of people. So I decided to leave the letter on the kitchen table and leave the door to the apartment unlocked. If anyone came in and found me, they would see the letter. Then I went back to the living room, sat down on the edge of the bed and picked up the envelope with the pills. I looked at the pills for a minute, put them down again, and went to the kitchen for a glass of water. Then I went back to the bed, took a swallow of water —and then took all the pills.

DR. SCHLESINGER

All at once?

JIM

I tried to. I emptied the pills from the envelope to my hand and took them all at one time. Several dropped on the floor and I even picked those up and took them, just to make sure.

DR. SCHLESINGER
(*As if the question had never been asked before*)
How many pills did you take?

JIM
(*Simply*)
A hundred and fifty-six.

62

DR. SCHLESINGER
(*His look says* JIM *is obviously lying*)
That's a strange number. How did you arrive at it?

JIM
(*His face is open—his tone honest*)
I didn't arrive at it, Doctor. That was the exact number.

DR. SCHLESINGER
How do you know?

JIM
I counted them. Sunday night, I put them on the kitchen table in groups of ten, and I counted them.

DR. SCHLESINGER
Why did you count them?

JIM
I had read in the papers several days before that some man had taken thirty-three pills and a lot of aspirin and all it did was to make him sick. I wanted to be sure I had enough.

DR. SCHLESINGER
I see. Where did you get the pills?

JIM
I bought them.

DR. SCHLESINGER
Where?

JIM

Different places—on Eighth Avenue.

DR. SCHLESINGER

Did you have prescriptions?

JIM

No. I had no trouble at all. I just asked for them.

DR. SCHLESINGER

Hm-hmmm. Now—to get back to that morning.

JIM

A week ago today, as a matter of fact. (*He smiles*) Strange, isn't it?

DR. SCHLESINGER

Yes—well—what happened after you took the pills?

JIM

Nothing. I was amazed. I didn't know what should happen, but nothing did.

DR. SCHLESINGER

What thoughts did you have at *that* time?

JIM

None. None at all.

DR. SCHLESINGER

You didn't think of anything? And yet, as far as you knew, you were dying.

JIM

I wondered whether I would have time now to mail the
letter to my brother.

DR. SCHLESINGER

Then, what did you do?

JIM

I mailed it—and I got quite a kick out of doing it. It
appealed to my sense of the dramatic, I guess. I walked down
the street to the mailbox on the corner, deposited the letter,
and walked back to the apartment. And all the time, I looked
at the people on the street—I said good morning to people
I knew—and I thought—they don't know it, but I'm a dying
man. When I got back to the house, I locked the door of my
apartment—I went into the living room, lay down on the
bed, folded my arms under my head and crossed my legs—
and then waited.

DR. SCHLESINGER

What did you think about then?

JIM

Nothing. I was comfortable. It seemed the most comfortable bed I'd ever known.

DR. SCHLESINGER

That's all?

JIM

I must have passed out about five or ten minutes later. It
wasn't longer—I'm pretty sure of that. My wife and the police
found me the next day. From what they tell me, it was just
about twenty-four hours after I had taken the pills.

DR. SCHLESINGER
(*Leans back again*)

Mr. Downs, what would you do if you got out of the hospital?

JIM
(*Frightened*)

I'd go home.

DR. SCHLESINGER

Back to your wife?

JIM
(*Unable to understand*)

We were separated. . . .

DR. SCHLESINGER

I know. But after all she has done for you. You don't know it, Mr. Downs, but you were kept on the critical list long after it was necessary, just to permit her to be with you.

JIM

I know. She told me.

DR. SCHLESINGER

She must love you very much.

JIM
(*This is a struggle*)

Doctor, this may make me out an awful heel. But you don't know my wife. She makes a terrific impression on everyone. Not only in the hospital. It's been that way for years.

Everybody thinks she's wonderful. I'm not trying to discount what she did for me here—but twenty-four-hours-a-day living together over a period of years is a completely different story.

DR. SCHLESINGER

If things are so difficult, why should she do—what she did for you?

JIM

This is going to sound even worse, but I can't help it. She wants to get me back, I suppose.

DR. SCHLESINGER

But why? Don't you think she loves you?

JIM
(*Slowly*)

Maybe. But the fear of loneliness is a better reason. One time, in a quarrel—I forget what it was about—for bringing only one salt and pepper shaker to the table instead of two, or dropping ashes on the floor—I forget now—I told her...

DR. SCHLESINGER
(*Interrupting*)

Just a minute. You quarreled about such things?

JIM

Oh, yes. She wouldn't talk to me for days after such an argument, dropping something—anything.

DR. SCHLESINGER

What did you tell her?

JIM

I told her she'd probably end up a lonely old woman. I think she's afraid of that. My wife is the same age as me—forty-two—and at that age the fear of loneliness can be a very real thing. She has a couple of friends—the only real friends she has, as a matter of fact—and they are alone. She knows what loneliness has done to these women. It's a terrible curse. I guess even having someone to fight with is better than being lonely.

DR. SCHLESINGER
(*A brief pause, pointedly*)

Then you don't think going back to your wife would mean a more stable life for you?

JIM

There was no stability before. Why should there be now? (*In reflection*) My wife's a very possessive woman. It took me a long time to get out of her clutches.

DR. SCHLESINGER
(*Quietly*)

Who is Charlotte?

JIM
(*Stunned*)

Charlotte?

DR. SCHLESINGER

Yes, Charlotte. Who is she?

JIM
(*Still shocked*)

A—a friend.

DR. SCHLESINGER

The friend who came to dinner that Saturday night?

JIM

Yes.

DR. SCHLESINGER
(*Toying with his pen*)

You tried to have a letter mailed to her. Didn't you know that was against the rules?

JIM

How did you know about the letter? Did Grosberg . . .

DR. SCHLESINGER

Yes, Mr. Grosberg gave me your letter. That's part of his job—keeping an eye on the patients. You must understand that when you are brought here for suicide you give up certain rights to privacy.

JIM

There was no harm in the letter. I just asked her to visit me, that's all. I can't understand why she hasn't been here.

DR. SCHLESINGER

Oh, she's been here all right, and she's been pestering me with phone calls. We haven't thought it wise for you to see her.

JIM

Who's we? My wife?

DR. SCHLESINGER

No, Dr. Barrow and myself. Are you involved with this girl?

JIM

How do you mean—involved?

DR. SCHLESINGER

Are you in love with her?

JIM

I don't know what you're getting at.

DR. SCHLESINGER

Do you *think* you're in love with her?

JIM

Well ...

DR. SCHLESINGER

Aren't my questions clear?

JIM

Yes, they are—but it seems like an awful lot of prying. If—if I'm well—I'd like to go home.

DR. SCHLESINGER

Why don't you want to answer my questions?

JIM

I'll co-operate in any way I can, Doctor, but I fail to see why Charlotte has to be brought into this.

DR. SCHLESINGER
(*Making a note*)

Hm-hmmmm.

JIM
(*While the doctor is writing*)
May I go home, Doctor? May I keep my appointment?

DR. SCHLESINGER

I'm afraid it may have to be postponed, Mr. Downs.

JIM

Why? For God's sake. This is the most vital appointment of my life.

DR. SCHLESINGER

I'm going to transfer you to another ward for a few days. Now, if you don't mind, look at my finger, please. (*He holds his index finger before* JIM's *eyes and moves it from left to right several times. Then, as he writes*) It's a convalescent ward, on the first floor. You'll like it. You can wear your own clothes there, instead of these hospital things. They play games down there—all sorts of interesting things. It's only for a few days.

JIM
(*Dazed, still sitting*)

I see.

DR. SCHLESINGER

That will be all, Mr. Downs.

(*Slowly* JIM *rises and goes.* DR. SCHLESINGER *goes on writing.*)

(*The lights fade quickly.*)

ACT ONE

Scene V

The whole ward.
Immediately following.
GROSBERG *sits on the bed of the staring one, whose nails*
he is filing.
FLEMING *is in bed.*
MISS HANSEN *is at the table.*

(JIM, *despondent, comes in and goes to his bed.*)

FLEMING

What's the matter, Downs?

JIM

Nothing.

FLEMING

Nothing! Christ, you look like . . .

JIM

I thought I was going home today.

FLEMING

What did he say?

JIM

I'm being transferred to the first floor—for a few days.

73

FLEMING

A few days, my foot. Everything around here's for a few days—the short way of saying indefinitely. You're going to "one." That's the observation ward. Nobody goes there for just a few days.

JIM
(*Quietly, not enjoying the remark*)
O.K. O.K.

FLEMING

You're in the psycho building, Downs. Didn't you know that?

JIM
(*Suddenly—as though struck*)
Psycho buil . . .

FLEMING

I guess you've been too sick to notice.

JIM

Notice what?

FLEMING

Look around you, for Christ's sake. Hey, Grosberg, tell this guy what MN 1 is like.

GROSBERG
(*To* JIM)
Is that where you're going?

JIM
(*Turns to him*)

Why did you turn in my letter? Why didn't you tell me first?

GROSBERG

I'm sorry—that's my job. (*He puts the file away, takes a comb from his pocket and combs the hair of the staring one*) You'll like it in "one," Mr. Downs. It's a convalescent ward. You can wear your own clothes. They play games down there and everything.

FLEMING

Grosberg, cut it out. Tell this guy where he's going.

GROSBERG
(*Softening the blow*)

It's not bad, really, Mr. Downs. It's the nicest ward. Lots of people go home from there.

JIM
(*Frightened*)

And if they don't go home?

GROSBERG
(*Quietly*)

State Hospital.

FLEMING

He didn't know he was in the psycho building.

75

GROSBERG

Oh, yes. Didn't you notice the windows, Mr. Downs? (*Goes to one*) This heavy screen in front? You see, you can't reach the window at all.

JIM

(*Dully*)

It never occurred to me.

GROSBERG

And the locked door? You didn't notice that?

JIM

Yes, I noticed it. I don't know why—it never occurred to me. Do all suicides come here?

GROSBERG

If they need medical care.

(*Returns to patient, combing hair.*)

JIM

Can you go right home from this ward?

GROSBERG

Yes, Mr. Downs, that's happened.

JIM

Then it isn't hospital procedure that a suicide is automatically sent to observation.

76

GROSBERG
(*A brief pause, simply*)

No.

(*The bell at the door rings once.*)

JIM
(*Cries out*)

But why? What did I say? What did I do?

GROSBERG

I don't know, Mr. Downs.

JIM

I told the truth about everything.

GROSBERG

I'm not the psychiatrist.

JIM

Can they keep me here—just like that—for no reason?

(*The door has been opened by* MISS HANSEN, *admitting* ANN.)

MISS HANSEN
(*Calls*)

Downs.

JIM
(*Turns. He sees* ANN *and runs to her, terror-stricken*)

Ann, they're putting me away. They think I'm insane.

ANN

It's only for a few days.

JIM
(*A step back*)

A few days?

ANN

What's the matter?

JIM
(*Horrified*)

You knew! (*He draws away from her. A chill runs through him as he looks at her*) You knew about this!

(*Curtain*)

ACT TWO

ACT TWO

SCENE I

Ward M N 1—City Hospital.

Essentially, it's the same ward we saw before. Structurally, it's exactly the same. But down here, the beds are made—all but one, which is bare but for the mattress.

The next day—Tuesday.

Some patients are wearing their own clothes; others are in hospital pajamas. No one wears a necktie, but more conspicuously, no one wears a belt. To hold his trousers up, regular or pajama trousers, each man is given a length of white gauze bandage.

SAM TAGER, *a Jewish boy, about twenty-seven, is sitting on his bed. He wears pajamas.* GEORGE O'BRIEN, *a small, thin, dark-complexioned boy of twenty, with kinky hair and a pronounced Spanish accent, is standing near him. Two beds away, to the left, is* JOHN ANKORITIS, *a swarthy Greek. He is reading a newspaper.* JOE MAJOR, *a powerfully built, but wonderfully graceful Negro, in his early thirties, is quietly drumming with his hands on the metal cabinet next to his bed.*

TAGER
(*Looking at a drawing, to* O'BRIEN, *quietly*)
Did you do this?

81

O'BRIEN

(*His Spanish accent is thick. He speaks rapidly*)

You like it? I never painted before in my life. You know who it is? The nurse with the smile. You know who I mean? The doctor say I should paint, I have ideas, I have talent. I like to paint.

TAGER

Where'd you get the name O'Brien?

O'BRIEN

My father, he was Irish. He left my mother before I was born.

TAGER

Where was this?

O'BRIEN

Havana, Cuba.

TAGER

Your mother alive?

O'BRIEN

No, she die when I am born. My aunt tell me everything when I grow up.

TAGER

(*Has been looking at drawings*)

Hey! *This* is good.

82

O'BRIEN

When I get out, I'm going to school, I get thousand dollar a picture when I learn.

(*Takes drawing back to his bed,* TAGER *shuffles a pack of cards aimlessly. The door is opened from the outside with a key, and* JIM DOWNS *enters, dressed as he was upstairs, followed by* DON GREGORY, *a tall, slender, young man of twenty-four.* GREGORY *is dressed in army sun-tans, the improvised uniform of an attendant. He carries* JIM'S *charts.* JIM *enters slowly, uncertain in every step.*)

GREGORY

(*Locks the door, turns to* JIM)

We'll find you a bed first, then I'll take these charts to the office. We're pretty crowded. We've got beds in the halls. (*To the men*) There's no bed in here, is there, fellows?

TAGER

Yeah, next to me.

GREGORY

Whose bed was it?

TAGER

O'Malley, the cop.

GREGORY

(*Surprised, he leads* JIM *to bed*)

Did he go home?

83

TAGER

Yeah, about an hour ago.

GREGORY

I'm glad for him. There's no pillow. I'll see if I can get you one. You have to keep your eyes open and grab one as soon as somebody leaves. Stay here for now, Mr. Downs. I'll get your linen. (*He starts to go, turns and looks at* JIM) And pajamas. Nobody's dressed like that down here. (*He leaves. A pause.*)

MAJOR
(*Looking at* JIM)

Your name Downs?

JIM
(*His eyes uncertain, bewildered. Quietly*)

Yes.

MAJOR

Mine's Major. Glad to know you.

(*He rises and shakes hands with* JIM *across* ANKORI-TIS' *bed.*)

TAGER
(*Simply waves to him*)

Sam Tager.

O'BRIEN
(*Also waving*)

George O'Brien.

84

ANKORITIS
(*Lying in bed*)

My name is John Ankoritis. I do not know how well versed you are in the sound of names, Mr. Downs, so I will tell you that I am Greek, and very proud of the heritage of my Hellenic ancestors.

JIM
(*Softly*)

You should be.

ANKORITIS
(*A broad smile*)

Thank you. We have a scholar in our midst, gentlemen. (*To* JIM) Would you like to see a copy of this morning's *Times*? It is at your disposal.

JIM

Thank you—I—I have a slight headache. Later, maybe.

ANKORITIS

May a thousand blessings descend upon your head, Mr. Major.

MAJOR

What for?

ANKORITIS

I have been in this pesthole for ten days and no one has ever thought to start introductions before. I like it. We must maintain the custom.

MAJOR

Just being friendly, that's all.

ANKORITIS

Excellent. Have a cigarette?

GREGORY

(*Enters with linen and pillow*)

I've got you a pillow. I'll help you make the bed. (*Throws open a sheet*) The fellows make their own beds every morning. Were you in the Army?

JIM

Yes.

GREGORY

Then you know how it is. Shaves three times a week. Showers every visiting day. (MAJOR *offers cigarette to* ANKORITIS, *takes one himself.* ANKORITIS *has the matches, and he lights* MAJOR'S *cigarette first, then his own.* GREGORY *sees the smoke. To* ANKORITIS *and* MAJOR) Now you fellows know you're not supposed to smoke in the ward. Go to the john or the day room—and give me the matches.

ANKORITIS

(*Throws him the matches.* GREGORY *puts them in his pocket*)

I have more.

GREGORY

Don't let me see them. You can always ask me for a light —you know that.

MAJOR

You're not always around.

(CARLISLE *enters. He is an old man, past sixty—a Negro, the gentlest man in the world, with a soft, slow voice. He goes to his bed, which is to the right, obviously in the hall.*)

GREGORY

Then ask one of the other attendants. You know I'm supposed to report this. Why do you do it? If someone else catches you, you'll wind up on "seven."

MAJOR
(*Laughing*)
You're always scaring us with "seven."

(*An authoritative voice off stage calls "Mr. Gregory!"*)

GREGORY

Watch out for your butts—will you, fellows? How are things, Mr. Carlisle?

CARLISLE

Fine—fine. (GREGORY *goes off.*) Them student nurses— they want to play cards all the time.

MAJOR

They're supposed to do that, Mr. Carlisle. That's their job.

87

CARLISLE

I know it's their job, but I don't want to play cards.

ANKORITIS

They want to engage you in conversation, my dear Mr. Carlisle.

CARLISLE
(*Gets under the covers*)

I know that.

ANKORITIS

They wish to extract information which they in turn pass on to the esteemed physicians.

CARLISLE
(*Gently*)

I know all that.

O'BRIEN

Everything you say and do down here gets reported.

TAGER

You ain't kidding. They don't miss a trick. Somebody's always watching you.

CARLISLE

I just want to be left alone. I don't like dominoes or Chinese checkers, or any games.

ANKORITIS

Then convey your displeasure in the most tactful manner, Mr. Carlisle.

CARLISLE

I did that—I told them I don't like to play games.

TAGER

That's the trouble in this place. Nobody treats you like a human being. You're a patient—you're being observed.

MAJOR

In here, we're special—everything we do has a meaning.

(TAGER *waves to* MAJOR *to play cards.* MAJOR *goes to* TAGER'S *bed.*)

O'BRIEN
(*Seriously*)

That's right. Just because you act a little crazy is no reason to say that you are.

ANKORITIS

It is the penalty, my dear Mr. O'Brien, of official surveillance. We lacked the wisdom to avoid being incarcerated.

O'BRIEN

Nobody sent *me* here. I came here by myself.

(CARLISLE *turns and looks at* O'BRIEN)

ANKORITIS

You're mad, my dear boy.

O'BRIEN

That's true. I knew I was run down, and a friend of mine told me I could come here for a physical check-up. He said ask any policeman and he will take you to the hospital. So I did, and he brought me to the hospital, and the nurse asked me what I wanted, and I told her a physical check-up, and they sent me here. That's the truth.

CARLISLE

Anybody walks in here by himself ought to go straight to "seven."

TAGER

Don't say that, Mr. Carlisle. You don't know what it's like on "seven."

JIM

(*Stops making his bed. He looks at* TAGER. *Finally summons the courage to ask*)
What's "seven"?

TAGER

The seventh floor. It's the violent ward. (JIM *stands still and listens*) I was in a straitjacket up there. I tried to throw myself in front of a subway train. Some cops grabbed me and I put up a fight—which I know now was a stupid thing to do. The next thing I know, I'm up on "seven" in a straitjacket. (*Seriously*) Did you see that movie, *The Snake Pit*? Well, they didn't exaggerate nothin'. My family saw it, and they said—aw, it's only a movie. They should know. Nobody knows till you see it from the inside. There was a guy up

90

there who used to dance on one foot and play the fiddle—an imaginary fiddle—like this . . . (*Rises and imitates him. The others watch soberly*) And there was one guy who used to go around as if he was looking in windows and he'd wave at somebody through the window—like this . . . (*Again the imitation*) You put that in a movie and people laugh. What's funny about that, will you tell me? (*A brief pause. They are quite serious*) I don't wish it on my worst enemy, they should go to "seven." (*He sits on his bed. The men are affected.* JIM *forces himself to go on making his bed.*)

SCHLOSS
(*A medium-sized gentleman from the "Greenpernt" section of Brooklyn enters in a hurry*)
Where's the new guy?

TAGER
(*Pointing*)
Right here.

SCHLOSS
I finished anudder chapter on my novel.

(*He goes to his cabinet to right of* TAGER'S *bed.*)

ANKORITIS
Doesn't the poetic muse inspire you any more, Mr. Schloss?

SCHLOSS
I'm finished wit' poetry. I'm writin' a novel. I got two chapters done since breakfast. (*To* JIM) What's your name?

91

JIM

Downs.

SCHLOSS

Mr. Downs, I hear you're in the theayter.

JIM

Where did you hear that?

SCHLOSS

It gets around fast. If you're in the theayter, you must be interested in literature. I want you should hear this here chapter. (*He reads from a dime-store tablet*) "So Captain Redbeard faces his bunch of cutthroats—the most villainous scoundrels that sailed the seven seas—and he says—Avast, me hearties, we are about to attack the good ship Avalon, which it is loaded with gold and silver from the Spanish Main." How do you like it?

JIM

You just started.

SCHLOSS

I mean, so far?

JIM

It's good.

SCHLOSS

The ideas just come to me, whereupon I write 'em. This here chapter's full of action.

JIM

It's good. You should continue.

SCHLOSS

That's what the doctor tells me. He says I got ideas—I just gotta learn some grammar, that's all. Would you believe it, I never did no writin' before?

ANKORITIS

This place must agree with, Mr.—eh—Mr.—eh . . .

SCHLOSS

Schloss is the name. No, this place stinks. It's worse than jail.

TAGER
(*Playing casino with* MAJOR)

Have you been to jail?

SCHLOSS

Sure. I give Uncle Sam two years in Leavenworth one time. And I give him eighteen months in Atlanta.

MAJOR

What do you mean, you *give* him?

SCHLOSS
(*Turns to him, angrily*)

He wanted it— so I gave it to him.

MAJOR

What for?

SCHLOSS

Defraudin' the govament. In jail, at least you know when you're gettin' out. In this God-damn place you never know nothin'. (*Turning the pages of his tablet*) Would you like to hear some of my poetry, Mr. Downs? "There is a nurse with smile so warm, but the smile conceals a heart so cold. She smiles so warm, it makes you bold, but then you find out her heart is cold." That's only the first voise. There's more.

TAGER

What are you doing in this ward, Mr. Schloss? There's nothing wrong with you.

SCHLOSS

Aaaaah, I slugged the wife and kids, so the cops trun me in here.

O'BRIEN

You should be ashamed to admit it, Mr. Schloss.

SCHLOSS
(*Without looking at him*)
You shut your mouth, you Spic bastard.

O'BRIEN
(*Rises*)

Take that back!

SCHLOSS
(*Rises*)

Ya lousy little bastard! Where do you come off with a name like O'Brien. Your mother was a Spic whore—that's what she was.

O'BRIEN
(*Fighting his tears*)

She was not. My mother was a good woman, she was a good . . . (*Sputters his rage*) You—You . . .

> (SCHLOSS *grabs* O'BRIEN's *shoulders and pushes him to floor.* ANKORITIS *goes to* SCHLOSS, *pulls him off.* CARLISLE *helps* O'BRIEN *to his feet.* TAGER *and* MAJOR *rise.*)

SCHLOSS

You take your crummy hands off me.

TAGER
(*Rushes between* SCHLOSS *and* ANKORITIS, *holding* ANKORITIS *away*)

Let him go, Mr. Ankoritis!

MAJOR
(*Furious, but staying clear of the fight*)

There ain't one of us here who wouldn't like to break Mr. Schloss's neck.

SCHLOSS

Yeah? Try it.

MAJOR
(*Takes step toward* SCHLOSS)

But we're the ones who'd wind up in "seven"—not him.

TAGER
(*Holds* MAJOR's *arm*)

Shut up, Mr. Major.

ANKORITIS

(*Quietly, with venom*)

It makes me sick to my stomach to look at you, Mr. Schloss.

SCHLOSS

(*Turns away*)

Aaah.

(*He goes to his bed.*)

GREGORY

(*Senses the silence as he enters*)

What happened?

TAGER

A few words.

GREGORY

Just keep it to words, boys—and no one will get hurt. Time for lunch, everybody. Let's go!

(*He starts to leave.*)

JIM

(*Anxiously—calls to him*)

Mr. Gregory. (GREGORY *stops and turns*) How soon can I see a doctor?

GREGORY

I don't know. They're way behind in interviews now.

JIM

How long do you think! I want to get out of here.

GREGORY

A few days maybe.

JIM

Before I even *see* a doctor?

GREGORY

It may be a few days before you're even assigned to a doctor. You'd better learn to be patient, Mr. Downs, if you want to get out of here. You start being anxious and you'll beat your head against the wall.

JIM
(*Furious*)

Oh, my God, why? Why? Why was I sent here in the first place?

GREGORY

There isn't a patient in this building who doesn't feel as you do.

JIM
(*Almost shouts*)

But I'm not—(*He stops suddenly in full realization, looks at* GREGORY *and then says quietly*) I see—no one else thinks he is, either.

GREGORY

That's right. In this place, *they* don't have to prove that you are—*you* have to prove that you're not. Chow, fellows. Are you all here?

(*He turns and leaves. The men ad-lib their response. They get up and start for the dining room.*)

ANKORITIS
(*As he leaves—with unconscious humor*)
You see, Mr. Downs, we are all *here,* but the question is, are we all *there?*

(JIM, *standing alone, slowly follows.*)

(*The lights fade quickly.*)

ACT TWO

SCENE II

*Once more, the lights pick out only a desk and two chairs—
the cubbyhole of an office. The rest of the stage is dark.*

The next day—Wednesday—after lunch.

DR. BELLMAN *is seated back of desk center. He is a young
man, not more than thirty-two or -three. He wears glasses.*

JIM *enters, wearing pajamas, top and bottom.*

DR. BELLMAN

Are you Mr. Downs?

JIM

Yes, sir.

DR. BELLMAN

Sit down, please.

JIM

Thank you.

DR. BELLMAN

How do you feel?

JIM

Fine.

DR. BELLMAN

Now tell me about this business.

99

JIM

The whole thing?

DR. BELLMAN

Whatever you want to say. Why did you do it?

JIM

Isn't it down in the chart? I gave all the details to Dr. Schlesinger.

DR. BELLMAN

I know—but I want you to tell *me*. What were the circumstances that morning?

JIM
(*Trying to be patient*)

The circumstances were that I was fed up with being out of work. I didn't think I was ever going to work again. My wife wanted money, and I figured the way to give it to her was to take my life.

DR. BELLMAN

Your G. I. insurance?

JIM

Yes.

DR. BELLMAN

How many pills did you take?

JIM

156. Why is that such a puzzler, Doctor? Everybody makes so much of that.

DR. BELLMAN
(*Ignores the question*)
How do you know there were exactly 156?

JIM
(*Rebuffed*)
I counted them.

DR. BELLMAN
Why?

JIM
Because I had read some guy had taken 33 pills and a load of aspirin, and it only made him sick. I wanted to be sure I had enough.

DR. BELLMAN
Do you frequently get periods of deep depression?

JIM
No, no more than most people.

DR. BELLMAN
I mean you, personally.

JIM
No.

DR. BELLMAN
Do you ever have periods of great elation?

JIM

I'm not manic-depressive, Doctor—if that's what these questions are intended to elicit.

DR. BELLMAN
(*Momentarily startled*)

Well, what exactly were you thinking about when you went through the preparation for this act?

JIM

Nothing—just what was happening at the moment.

DR. BELLMAN

Don't you think that's strange?

JIM

Not at all. It was a conscious decision. I made up my mind to do it, and that was that.

DR. BELLMAN

Didn't you think of how other people would feel when they found out?

JIM

No, I'm not really that important to anyone.

DR. BELLMAN

Didn't you think your wife would be hurt?

JIM

Not really. She'd have gotten over it very quickly.

DR. BELLMAN

And—Charlotte?

JIM

Well—yes—but it wouldn't last. No such hurt lasts, except as an affectation.

DR. BELLMAN

Why do you say that?

JIM

It's true. (*He laughs*) The world would soon come to a stop if all the dead were continually mourned.

DR. BELLMAN
(*Looks at* JIM *a moment*)

I see. (*A brief pause*) Do you know you have a reputation for being belligerent and nasty?

JIM
(*Puzzled*)

I have?

DR. BELLMAN

Yes.

JIM

I'm sorry, Doctor. I had always thought of myself as an easy person to get along with. I think my friends would say that about me.

DR. BELLMAN

Maybe they don't know you well enough.

JIM

May I ask—who told you I had such a reputation?

DR. BELLMAN

People who know you well.

JIM

But who can they be?

DR. BELLMAN

Your wife knows you well, doesn't she?

JIM
(*Slowly*)

Yes. I suppose.

DR. BELLMAN

Is it true?

JIM

Well, that's hardly for me to say, is it? I'm sorry she feels that way.

DR. BELLMAN

Your wife says, also, you are frequently wild and incoherent.

JIM
(*Disturbed*)

I'm wild and incoherent? Honest to God!

DR. BELLMAN

What's the matter, Mr. Downs?

JIM

Either you're making this up to see how I'll behave, or something has happened to my wife. We were separated, I know, but I can't believe she'd say such things about me.

DR. BELLMAN

Then you don't think it's true?

JIM

Of course it's not true.

DR. BELLMAN

Tell me about Charlotte, will you?

JIM

She's a girl I fell in love with. Now is that so unusual?

DR. BELLMAN

What sort of a girl is she?

JIM
(*Beginning to lose control*)

Look, Dr. Bellman, I'll answer any question you like about the attempt on my life—I *have* answered—as completely as I can—all your questions. But Charlotte has nothing to do with this.

DR. BELLMAN

You must allow me to decide that, Mr. Downs.

JIM

I want to go home. I'm perfectly well now.

DR. BELLMAN
(*Quietly*)

In time, Mr. Downs. You must have patience. Everyone in the hospital speaks very well of your wife. She was extremely devoted in your first critical days here.

JIM

I know. Everybody tells me Ann is a fine person.

DR. BELLMAN

Did you ever try to give up Charlotte?

JIM

A dozen times. I didn't want to hurt Ann. I tried to go on living with her. That only made it worse. I was miserable with Charlotte and I was miserable at home.

DR. BELLMAN

So you finally took your own apartment?

JIM

Yes.

DR. BELLMAN

How long were you living alone before this happened?

JIM

About three months.

DR. BELLMAN
(*Making notes*)

I see.

JIM

I've answered your questions, Doctor. May I go home?

DR. BELLMAN
(*Still writing*)

Just a minute.

JIM

I don't belong here—you can see that.

DR. BELLMAN

Of course. Just a few more questions. Who's the mayor of New York?

JIM
(*At once*)

Impellitteri.

DR. BELLMAN

Who's the President of the United States?

JIM

Truman.

DR. BELLMAN

Who was the President before him?

JIM

Roosevelt.

107

DR. BELLMAN

When did President Roosevelt die?

JIM

(*Looks at* BELLMAN, *incredulously*)

Doctor—you don't really think I'm insane, do you?

DR. BELLMAN

Just answer my questions—when did Roosevelt die?

JIM

April—April—(*A pause*) April—12th—1945.

DR. BELLMAN

What is the capital of France?

JIM

Paris.

DR. BELLMAN

What does the expression—a rolling stone gathers no moss—mean to you?

JIM

Well—it means that—a person who wanders around a great deal doesn't plant any roots—has no foundation—doesn't gather any of the moss of well-being, if you want to put it that way—of stability.

DR. BELLMAN

I see. And the expression—people who live in glass houses shouldn't throw stones?

JIM

That means—people of equal guilt, for the same fault, perhaps—shouldn't hurl accusations at each other.

DR. BELLMAN

Hm-hmm. Now subtract by sevens from a hundred.

JIM

You've finally hit a weak spot.

DR. BELLMAN

Go ahead.

JIM
(This is slow and painful)
Ninety-three—eighty-four—seventy-seven—seventy—sixty-three—fifty—fifty-six—forty-nine—forty-two—thirty-five—twenty-eight—twenty-one—fourteen—seven—zero. (JIM *is agitated*) I want to tell you a story, Doctor.

DR. BELLMAN

What is it?

JIM
(He knows he is saying the wrong thing, but seems driven by some relentless force)
Four years ago I knew a doctor—a young psychiatrist in exactly your position— attached at that time to another City Hospital. He wanted me to write a play with him based on some of his case histories. One day, while he was making the rounds, he stopped in this screened-in porch, and he asked

109

one of the patients—what day is today? The girl didn't answer, and he said—do you know who I am? She still didn't answer, but I could see the disgust in her face. Then one of the other patients answered—an older woman. She turned around and said—(*Imitating the sarcasm in a high voice*) Who's the Mayor of New York? Who's the Governor of the State? Who's the President of the United States?

DR. BELLMAN
(*Confused for a moment*)
Well, what does that prove?

JIM
To me, Doctor—particularly since—ironically—I find myself four years later in exactly the same position—it proves that institutional practice and honesty are not compatible.

DR. BELLMAN
Why do you say that?

JIM
We should be treated as individuals, but we're handled in categories—the same routine for everyone. What is it, Doctor—inexperience? Lack of time?

DR. BELLMAN
I can't discuss that with you, Mr. Downs.

JIM
That woman wound up in the violent ward for her pains. What will happen to me?

DR. BELLMAN

We'll see. Stand up, Mr. Downs. (JIM *does*) Hold your arms out with your fingers extended. All right—now close your eyes. (JIM *stands that way for nearly a minute*) All right. Now look at my finger. (*He moves his finger from left to right several times*) All right. That's all for now.

JIM

When do I go home?

DR. BELLMAN
(*Firmly*)

You don't, Mr. Downs. Not for a while.

(*The lights fade quickly.*)

ACT TWO

Scene III

The ward.

Close to nine P.M.—*the same day.*

It is near bedtime and lights out. Those who were in street clothes have changed to pajamas.

CARLISLE *fusses with his bed, mumbling quietly to himself.* SCHLOSS *is sitting up and writing, using his drawn-up knees as a desk.*

JIM *is sitting on his bed.* ANKORITIS *is standing to the right of* JIM. TAGER *is sitting on his bed facing* JIM. O'BRIEN *and* MAJOR *are sitting on* TAGER's *bed.*

TAGER

The theatre must be a fascinating business, Mr. Downs.

O'BRIEN

Who do you know, Mr. Downs—any movie stars?

ANKORITIS

Of course, the theatre originated in Greece.

TAGER

It did, Mr. Downs?

ANKORITIS

Everybody knows that.

TAGER
(*To* JIM)
Is that right, Mr. Downs?

ANKORITIS
(*Offended*)
You question my veracity?

TAGER
If Mr. Downs says so, it's all right. He's a professional. . . .

(MISS WINGATE *enters the ward. She is tall, heavy, middle-aged, unintelligent, and has the broadest possible Southern accent.*)

MISS WINGATE
Bedtime, boys. Nine o'clock.

O'BRIEN
(*To* JIM—*eagerly*)
Do you know any movie stars?

JIM
I've met a few.

MISS WINGATE
Get to bed, boys. It's nine o'clock. Light's going out. I can't stand here all night. I've got work to do.

(*The group breaks up. Everyone gets into bed.* O'BRIEN *follows* JIM.)

114

O'BRIEN

Who do you know?

MISS WINGATE

O'Brien, your bed's not over there. Now get into bed.

O'BRIEN

Yes, Miss Wingate.

(*He scurries back to his own bed.*)

MISS WINGATE

Now I don't want to hear any noise from this ward. You boys keep the whole floor awake with your noise at night and I'm not going to stand for any more noise. Do you hear?

O'BRIEN

Good night, Miss Wingate.

MISS WINGATE

Don't you tell me good night.

ANKORITIS

Good night, Miss Wingate.

MISS WINGATE

Who was that—Ankorītis?

ANKORITIS

Yes, Miss Wingate—and it's pronounced Ankorītis. It is a name, not a disease.

115

MISS WINGATE
(*Furious*)

Is that so? Well, you'd just better be careful how you talk to me, Ankoritis, or you'll wind up in "seven"—and I don't think you'd like that.

TAGER

Would you put the lights out, please, Miss Wingate? I want to get to sleep.

MISS WINGATE

You get to sleep, Mr. Tager, and I'll put the lights out when I get good and ready. You boys think you're smart. The whole lot of you will wind up in "seven" if you're not careful. Seventy-two patients in this ward and you men are the worst.

O'BRIEN

Good night, Miss Wingate.

ANKORITIS

May your repose in the arms of Morpheus be a pleasant one, Miss Wingate.

MISS WINGATE

Thank you. Good night.

(*She goes, after putting out the ward lights with a key. The switch panel is near the door.*)

O'BRIEN
(*Calls softly from his bed*)

Mr. Downs—what movie stars do you know?

JIM
(*Quietly*)

I'll tell you tomorrow.

(*A pause.*)

CARLISLE

Well—another day—another dollar.

(*A pause.*)

MAJOR
(*Quietly—from his bed*)

You can make up the dollar—but you can't make up the day. In this place—it's just gone.

(*A pause.*)

O'BRIEN
(*Softly*)

Do you know Betty Grable?

SCHLOSS
(*In a tense whisper*)

Shut up, for Christ's sake! You ever got near Betty Grable you'd wet your pants.

O'BRIEN
(*Just as tense a whisper—the effect, back and forth is of a continuous hiss*)

Is that so?

SCHLOSS

Yeah—that's so.

O'BRIEN

In Havana one time I saw ...

SCHLOSS

In Havana your mother was a whore. ...

O'BRIEN

I'll break your neck!

SCHLOSS

You threatened me. (*Suddenly yells*) Miss Wingate! (*He throws the covers off and jumps out of bed*) Miss Wingate! (*He runs into the corridor—the other men sit up in their beds*) Miss Wingate!

TAGER

Keep your mouth shut, Mr. Schloss!

MAJOR

Aw, forget it, Mr. Schloss.

Together

CARLISLE

Leave him alone.

(MISS WINGATE *appears.*)

SCHLOSS

He threatened me, Miss Wingate.

MISS WINGATE

Who?

SCHLOSS
Mr. O'Brien. He said he'd break my neck.

MISS WINGATE
He did? (*She goes into the ward*) O'Brien, did you say you were going to break Mr. Schloss's neck? O'Brien, are you in your bed? Well, I'll soon find out. (*She goes to entrance and turns the lights on.* O'BRIEN *is standing against the wall near his bed, hysterical with fear*) Did you hear me talking to you, Mr. O'Brien? You know what happens to people who make threats down here. (*All the men are watching in helpless rage*) Mr. Schloss, get the attendants—I'll call the doctor in a minute.

(SCHLOSS *goes off.*)

TAGER
Miss Wingate—Mr. Schloss was responsible. . . .

MISS WINGATE
I don't want to hear a word out of any of you. No point asking you, O'Brien, whether you threatened Mr. Schloss. Of course, you'll deny it.

O'BRIEN
(*Through wild sobbing*)
He—he—said my mother—he—insulted my mother.

MISS WINGATE
I don't care what he said about your mother. You can't go around threatening people. When you get to "seven" you won't be able to threaten anybody. (*Two attendants enter*) Here he is—take him up. I'll call the doctor.

119

O'BRIEN
(*Falls to his knees, crying*)
Don't take up to "seven"—please don't take me to "seven"!
(*The attendants take his arms—he is so much smaller than they, there is practically no resistance—but the cries are more piercing as they take him away*) Please don't take me to "seven"! Please don't take me to "seven"!

MISS WINGATE
(*Locks the door and puts out the lights*)
Now all you men get back to sleep. I don't want to hear another word—d'you hear? Get to sleep, all of you. Land a'mercy, I don't know how I'm going to get my work done with all this going on. (SCHLOSS *goes to bed. She sits at desk*) Oh, Mr. Downs—you asleep?

JIM
(*From his bed*)
No.

MISS WINGATE
There's a telegram for you. Been here for a while, but I've just been so busy I haven't had time to even think about it.

JIM
(*Still shocked by what happened*)
Thank you, Miss Wingate.

MISS WINGATE
(*After a pause*)
Well? Don't you want it?

120

JIM
(*Slowly*)

Yes—yes, of course.

(*He gets out of bed and goes to her.*)

MISS WINGATE

Here it is. (*She takes telegram from her pocket*) You can read it at the desk. You'll have to show it to me when you're finished.

JIM
(*Takes the telegram, holds it a moment*)

Miss Wingate—that O'Brien boy . . .

MISS WINGATE

Never mind about that O'Brien boy. What does the telegram say? (JIM *goes to the desk, reads the telegram, then hands it to* MISS WINGATE. *She reads aloud*) Darling, you must tell the doctors you want to see me—otherwise am not permitted—I love you—Charlotte. Well, who's this Charlotte?

JIM

Isn't it plain enough?

MISS WINGATE

But you have a wife, haven't you?

JIM
(*Exasperated*)

We were separated, Miss Wingate—for three months, before this happened.

MISS WINGATE

Well, I don't care how long you're separated. You're still married, aren't you?

JIM

Yes.

MISS WINGATE

You have a wife and a girl friend?

JIM

That's hardly the way to put it. . . .

MISS WINGATE

I don't care how you put it—with a wife and a girl friend —you'll never get out of here. Have you seen this girl since you've been here?

JIM

You saw the telegram.

MISS WINGATE

Well, my advice to you is to write this girl tonight.

JIM

But . . .

MISS WINGATE

No buts, Mr. Downs. I'm trying to help you. The law recognizes only the wife—so get used to it. What are you trying to do—break down the sanctity of marriage?

JIM

Miss Wingate, I . . .

MISS WINGATE

Your wife can get you out of here if she wants to.

JIM
(*His thought arrested*)

She can?

MISS WINGATE

We can't hold you, Mr. Downs, if she wants to take you home.

JIM

You sure about that?

MISS WINGATE

Of course I'm sure. That's the law. It happens all the time. So if I were you I would tell this girl you don't want to see her again. I'll give you paper and pencil. Here—you write it right now and I'll mail it for you.

JIM
(*Takes paper and pencil*)

Suppose I just say—don't try to see me—I'll explain when I get out.

MISS WINGATE
(*Thinks about it*)

Well, what happens outside is none of my business. I guess it's all right.

123

JIM

Thank you—(*He starts to write, then stops*) Miss Wingate—that O'Brien boy really didn't do anything. . . .

MISS WINGATE

Now, Mr. Downs, you keep your nose clean.

JIM

But is it possible—without proof—without knowing who's right or who's wrong—to . . .

MISS WINGATE

I'm trying to help you, Mr. Downs. Just you write your little note and stay out of anybody else's business. You got your own problems to worry about.

JIM

(*Looks at her, finishes the note and gives it to her*)
Thank you, Miss Wingate.

(*He goes back to bed.*)

(*A moment's pause, then very quietly* MR. CARLISLE *gets out of bed.*)

CARLISLE

(*Gently shakes the front of* TAGER's *bed*)
Come on, boys, get up. (*Goes to* JIM's *bed*) My daughter's comin' home—she won't like it, she catch you here. (*Shakes* ANKORITIS' *bed*) Now, come on, boys—please. Get your clothes on and go home. My daughter won't like it at all, she find you here. (*Goes to* MISS WINGATE) Time for these boys to be gettin' on home—my daughter . . .

MISS WINGATE

(*Takes* CARLISLE *by the arm. Her voice is soft—it can be on occasion*)

Now you go to bed, Mr. Carlisle. I'll take care of your daughter when she comes.

(*She walks him back to his bed.*)

CARLISLE

(*Always gentle*)

You will? Thank you. (*Peacefully, he gets into bed*) My daughter's very funny that way. Good night, Miss Wingate.

MISS WINGATE

(*Quietly*)

Good night, Mr. Carlisle.

(*She fixes his covers as he goes to sleep.*)

(*The lights fade quickly.*)

ACT TWO

Scene IV

The same.
The next day—Thursday—2:00 P.M.
As the lights come up the bell at the door is heard. JIM *is alone in the ward, sitting on his bed.* GREGORY *crosses the stage from right to left and unlocks the door.* ANN *is there.*

GREGORY

These aren't visiting hours.

ANN
(*Handing him pass*)

I have a special pass.

GREGORY
(*Looks at it—then at* ANN)

I'll have to examine your package.

ANN

Certainly.

(*She gives him the bag of fruit.*)

GREGORY
(*After examining package*)

O.K.

(*He lets her pass, then goes off.*)

127

ANN
(*Goes to* JIM's *bed*)

Jim . . .

JIM
(*Has watched what happened. He is waiting*)

Ann . . .

ANN

Well, you look fine. Much better than you did, upstairs.

JIM

Hm-hmmm.

ANN

I brought you some fruit and some chocolate.

JIM

(*Takes package and goes to cabinet beside his bed*)

Thanks, Ann. I was going to ask you. Most of the fellows pretty much share what they get.

ANN

I'll bring more next time.

JIM

I'm hoping there won't be a next time.

ANN

What did your new doctor say?

JIM

Do you know him?

ANN

I haven't met him. I've spoken to him on the phone. He sounds nice.

JIM

He said I'd have to stay awhile. Ann, I want to get out of here.

ANN

Of course, dear. I'm doing everything I can.

JIM

You can get me out on your say-so. You can do it, Ann— if you want to.

ANN

Of course I want to. But it isn't as simple as all that.

JIM

It is, Ann. I've learned that. The night nurse told me.

ANN

Well, I don't know what she told you, but I spoke to Dr. Bellman this morning on the phone, and he said you'll have to stay awhile.

JIM
(*Stares at her. A brief pause*)
Ann, are you trying to have me committed?

ANN

That's silly, dear. You're upset. I can understand that.

JIM

(*Becoming more and more agitated*)

No, you can't understand. I am the one behind locked doors, not you. You can come and go as you like. Every day I stand at the barred window and hear those boat whistles and automobile horns, and the sounds spell freedom, but I'm not free.

ANN

You will be, dear.

JIM

Don't pretty it up, Ann. You don't know what goes on here. I've seen fears built up in these men that didn't exist before. I don't know why most of them are here, but after they spend a day in this place, those fears take over.

ANN

How do you know that?

JIM

I know, because it's happening to me. I want to go home, Ann.

ANN

What sort of fears?

JIM

(*Almost angrily*)

"Seven"—and the green slip. You should hear the men talking about them.

ANN

They must be hospital terms. What do they mean?

JIM

"Seven" is the violent ward and the green slip is commitment to a state hospital.

ANN

Well, that's not going to happen to you.

JIM

It can. It can. I've seen it happen on the flimsiest pretext. You've got to hold on tight to keep your balance here, Ann. Everything you say and do is reported. You are constantly watched. I shouldn't even be getting so excited now. If I'm seen, it will set me back God knows how long. You can't have normal feelings here, Ann. Only continuous calm. Is that normal—for anyone?

ANN

You're exaggerating, dear.

JIM

Exaggerating? My God, how can I make you understand?

ANN

I tell you you're not being committed.

JIM

How do you know?

ANN

I had a long talk with Dr. Davidson. . . .

JIM

Davidson! What did you go to see him about?

ANN

I think you'll be pleased. I thought if our own doctor—he's known the two of us for eight years or more—would intercede . . .

JIM
(*Impatiently*)

Fine—fine. What's he going to do?

ANN

He has some influence with the Veterans Administration, and he thought maybe he could get you into a Veterans Hospital.

JIM
(*Almost shouts*)

No! I want to go home!

ANN
(*Quietly*)

Hush, Jim.

JIM
(*His voice lower, but still intense*)

I don't want any hospital. I want to go home. I'm not a mental case. Do you think I'm a mental case?

ANN

No, Jim, of course not. But Davidson thought you might need psychiatric help—after what you did.

JIM

What I did is over—I'm alive now. I'm no more ill than you are. But I don't seem able to convince anybody. (*The briefest pause*) Ann, why did you tell Dr. Bellman I was belligerent and nasty.

ANN

Why did I what?

JIM

Was I ever belligerent to you?

ANN

No, dear.

JIM

And you told him that at times I was wild and incoherent.

ANN
(*Starts to cry*)
I don't know why he would tell you those things, Jim, I . . .

JIM

How are you helping me, Ann, if you tell the doctor I'm belligerent and nasty—and wild and incoherent?

ANN

You don't give me a chance to explain.

JIM

What can you say? I hardly think he made it up.

133

ANN

When you say things like that, I think Davidson's right.

JIM

(*Quickly*)

Then you do think I'm sick?

ANN

I didn't say that.

JIM

Ann, I warn you—if I get a green slip, I'll fight it. I'll fight it in court. You're allowed to, you know. The court sits right here in this building.

ANN

You don't have to fight me!

JIM

Then why aren't you trying to get me out, instead of talking about my going to another hospital?

ANN

We thought it was best. . . .

JIM

If I need help, I can get it outside.

ANN

We can't afford it, Jim. Private psychiatrists are so expensive.

134

JIM

I can go to a clinic—I can go to the V.A., but I'll be free—
I'll be home—I won't be confined in an institution. I lie
awake at night—and they know it because they walk through
the ward three or four times a night with a flashlight. If you
sleep, that's good—if you don't sleep, that's a sign of nervous-
ness. Last night I pretended to sleep, and this morning the
nurse said—I'm glad you're feeling better, Mr. Downs.

ANN
(*Pause*)

What do you want me to do?

JIM
(*In tears, helplessly*)

I had thought of reaching Davidson myself, but now it
turns out he thinks I belong here. . . .

ANN

He doesn't think that. . . . He thinks you need help.

JIM
(*Urgently*)

Then tell him to come down here and see Dr. Bellman.
And get Dr. Walker—he's a phychiatrist, he knows the routine—he's the one who wanted me to write a play with him.
They've got to come down here—just phoning the hospital is
not enough. Tell them I'll pay them for their time, if that's
necessary. I'll get the money some way. But they've got to
come down here—tomorrow.

135

ANN

All right, I'll call them.

JIM

You can't just ask them please, will you do it? You've got
to make them see how important it is.

ANN

I will. I will, dear.

(DR. BELLMAN *enters.*)

DR. BELLMAN
(*Goes to* JIM)

Is this your wife, Mr. Downs?

JIM

Yes. Ann, this is Dr. Bellman.

ANN

How do you do?

DR. BELLMAN

I'd like to see you for a minute, Mrs. Downs.

ANN
(*Starts to go*)

Certainly.

DR. BELLMAN

No, take your time. When you've spoken to your husband.
(*To* JIM) How do you feel?

JIM

(*Turns his head away so the doctor will not see his tears. Mutters*)

Fine. (DR. BELLMAN *goes to the desk and sits down*) Maybe you'd better speak to him now.

ANN

In a minute. He's busy now. Jim, is it true you tried to reach Charlotte?

JIM
(*Stunned*)

Why?

ANN

Now don't pretend. Dr. Schlesinger told me.

JIM
(*In a trap*)

Is—is that so unnatural?

ANN

No. I just wanted to know how you felt.

JIM

Well, Ann, it's no secret that . . .

ANN

It's also no secret that I've done a great deal for you since you came to the hospital.

JIM

I know, Ann. Everyone's told me.

ANN

Oh, before I forget. Would you endorse this for me?

(*Takes check from her purse.*)

JIM

What's this?

ANN

The check for your teaching. Endorse it to me.

JIM

But I won't have a nickel when I get out of the hospital.

ANN

I'm not asking anything for myself. There are bills to pay
—money for the special nurses, and God knows what else.
They're all your expenses.

JIM
(*Helplessly*)

Yes, Ann.

ANN
(*Gives him pen*)

Here. (JIM *endorses the check and returns the pen.* ANN
puts check in her purse) I'd better see Dr. Bellman now.

JIM

Yes.

ANN
(*As she puts on her coat*)

Oh, I spoke to Mr. Williams for you. It's too bad you couldn't make that appointment. He had just about settled on you for the job.

JIM
(*Dumbly*)

He had?

ANN

That should make you feel good—to know that he wanted you.

JIM

Yes, it does.

ANN

I'd better see Dr. Bellman now. (*She takes a few steps and turns*) I'll see you Saturday. Take care, dear.

JIM

Thanks. Oh, Ann . . . (*Takes step toward her*) You have my keys?

ANN

Yes.

JIM

Bring some clothes for me, will you? These things . . .

(*He fingers the pajamas.*)

ANN

Of course—Saturday.

(*She starts toward* BELLMAN.)

JIM
(*Turns and calls again to* ANN)

Ann . . .

ANN

Yes?

JIM

Ask Dr. Bellman whether you can get me out on your own, will you?

ANN

Of course.

JIM

You won't forget?

ANN

No, dear. (JIM *goes silently off.* ANN *reaches* DR. BELL-MAN) Dr. Bellman?

DR. BELLMAN
(*Gets up from the desk*)

Mrs. Downs.

ANN

They certainly keep you busy.

DR. BELLMAN
(*Attempting to smile*)

Well, I wish I could spend more time with the men's fami-
lies. I could learn a lot more about the men themselves. But
...

(*He shrugs his shoulders.*)

ANN

I understand.

DR. BELLMAN

What do you think?

ANN

About Jim? He frightens me—the things he says.

DR. BELLMAN

He shows quite a bit of antagonism and resentment. I don't
think he's telling the complete truth yet. There are many
questions he refuses to answer.

ANN

Dr. Bellman, he's afraid of being committed.

DR. BELLMAN
(*Alert*)

Did he say that?

ANN

Yes. Is it possible he may be committed?

141

DR. BELLMAN

There are several possibilities, Mrs. Downs. He can be discharged in your custody—if you want to assume that responsibility.

ANN

I'd gladly assume that responsibility, Doctor. But if he isn't well enough . . .

DR. BELLMAN

He may be committed to a State Hospital.

ANN

I see. He wants me to reach several doctor friends on the outside. What do you think?

DR. BELLMAN

I wouldn't suggest it.

ANN

You know best, Doctor. Thank you.

DR. BELLMAN

Not at all. Now if you'll forgive me?

(*He walks to the left to open the door for* ANN.)

ANN

Certainly.

(*She starts for the door.*)

(*The lights fade quickly.*)

ACT TWO

SCENE V

The same.
Five days later—Tuesday.
JOE MAJOR *is singing a calypso song and drumming its*
rhythm on the **table down left**. ANKORITIS *is seated opposite*
him. TAGER *is standing between them. All three are singing,*
though MAJOR *is the expert. They are having fun.* JIM *is*
sitting alone, on his bed. SCHLOSS *is sitting on his bed, writ-*
ing. CARLISLE *is asleep in his bed.*

TAGER
(*After a moment of the singing*)
Come over here, Mr. Downs. You'll like this.

MISS WINGATE
(*Enters and goes to* CARLISLE's *bed*)
Time for your medicine, Mr. Carlisle.

(CARLISLE *resists getting up.* WINGATE *throws his*
covers off.)

JIM
(*Looks up and sees* WINGATE)
Miss Wingate . . .

MISS WINGATE
I'm busy.

143

JIM
(*Goes to her*)
Can I have . . . (*He turns to the men drumming and singing*) Please—fellows—hold it down—hold it down . . . (*The men look at him strangely, and soften their singing. He turns back to* MISS WINGATE) Can I have an appointment with Dr. Bellman?

MISS WINGATE
(*Getting* CARLISLE *out of bed*)
You had your interview with him, didn't you?

JIM
Yes.

MISS WINGATE
He'll call you if he wants to talk to you again.

JIM
But I want to . . .

(MISS WINGATE *leaves with* CARLISLE *without bothering to answer.* JIM *is left standing. The volume of drumming and singing increases. He turns to the men —bothered by the noise—then starts for his bed.*)

GREGORY
(*Enters left and starts collecting dominoes, checkers, magazines, etc.*)
You fellows are not supposed to take these games out of the day room—you know that.

JIM
(Turns to GREGORY)

Don ...

GREGORY

Sloppiest bunch of guys I ever saw.

JIM
(Goes to him)

Don, do I get another appointment with Bellman?

GREGORY

He'll call you, Jim. Have you had any tests?

JIM

I took the Rorschach yesterday.

GREGORY

It'll take at least a week for the results of that to come through.

> *(It makes no difference whether we hear these lines or not.* JIM *cannot stand much more of the noise and, as he talks, keeps turning to the men.)*

JIM
(Finally shouts at them—violently)

For God's sake, fellows, you're not the only ones in this ward.

GREGORY
(Goes to him)

Take it easy, Jim.

JIM

(*Looks at him savagely.* GREGORY *seems no longer his friend*)

You, too. Take it easy. Take it easy.

(*He turns away.*)

GREGORY

(*Takes* JIM's *arm*)

Lie down awhile, Jim. Try to relax. (JIM *wrenches away —goes to the drumming group—suddenly kicks the table, knocking it over.* GREGORY *grabs him, pinning his arms*) What do you think you're doing? Do you know what would happen if I reported this?

JIM

(*Still struggling*)

Report it! Go ahead and report it! I don't want any favors.

GREGORY

(*Shouts*)

Jim! (*He tightens his grip on* JIM's *arms.* JIM *quiets down*) Come here, Jim. Sit down.

(*He takes him to a bed.*)

JIM

(*Almost crying*)

Why are they keeping me? What have I done? I hurt no one but myself. Until I took the pills nobody questioned me. Nobody stopped me on the street as if I were a suspicious character. Well, I'm still the same guy. What's the difference now?

GREGORY

The difference is that you took the pills.

JIM

But . . .

GREGORY

What's the difference between a guy just holding a gun
and a guy that pulls the trigger? The fact that he did it. . . .

JIM
(*Holds his head*)

Christ, Don, I don't want any riddles. Why are they keeping me?

GREGORY
(*Kneels to him, patiently*)

Listen to me, Jim. The doctors take most cases of suicide
to be an inverted homicidal tendency. Do you know what that
means? (JIM *raises his head and looks at* GREGORY. GREGORY
explains) You're a potential murderer in their eyes, even
though you only tried to kill yourself. (JIM *looks wordlessly
at* GREGORY. GREGORY *stands up, pats him gently on the
shoulder. He walks toward the group at the table. He turns
back to look at* JIM *and then nods to the group*) O.K., fellows. But take it easy.

> (*He goes off. The men in the group look at* JIM.
> JOE MAJOR *starts another calypso song quietly. Soon
> the tempo increases and the others join in. The vol-
> ume swells, and the men are no longer giving their
> attention to* JIM. *He sits forlornly, looking at them.*

Slowly, he turns to the window. He gets up from the bed, takes a step to the window, and his head falls pathetically to one side. The drumming and singing have reached a crescendo.)

(*Curtain*)

ACT THREE

ACT THREE

The dining room.
Two days later. Thursday. About 1:30 P.M.
It is visiting day, but early. There is no one in the corridor and no visitors are at the door.
GREGORY is unlocking the door. ANN and HARRY DOWNS, JIM's brother, take a step inside. He is a small-town business-man.

ANN

Show him your pass, Harry (*To* GREGORY) This is Mr. Downs' brother.

GREGORY

(*Takes the pass from* DOWNS *and reads it carefully, then looks at him briefly*)
Will you have a seat? (*Turns to* ANN) I'll call him.

ANN

Thank you.
(GREGORY *goes off.* ANN *and* HARRY DOWNS *go to a table. It is obvious that* HARRY *is aware of the place he is in. He moves as though he were afraid to do the wrong thing*)
This is the dining room.

151

HARRY
(*Looking around, nods his head*)
Hm-hmmm.

ANN
He forgot to look in my package. They examine everything
before they let you in.

HARRY
Do you see all kinds—I mean, the violent ones, too?

ANN
No. They're on a different floor. This is only the observation ward.

HARRY
Why was he sent here?

ANN
(*Disturbed—looks at* DOWNS)
You know what he did.

HARRY
I know—but hundreds of people have tried the same thing.
They don't wind up in a—in a . . .

(*He is almost afraid to name the place.*)

ANN
This isn't that kind of place, really.

(JIM *enters right. He hasn't slept and his eyes show
it. He seems almost as uncertain as he did when he*

152

*first came to "one." He sees his brother and stops. A
strange embarrassment comes over him at the realization of where they are meeting.)*

JIM
(Quietly)

Hello, Harry.

HARRY

How do you feel?

JIM

All right. When did you get here?

HARRY

I flew in from Pittsburgh this morning. I had a few errands
to do when I got to the City, then I called Ann.

JIM
(To HARRY)

Why did it take you so long to get here?

HARRY

What do you mean?

JIM

I've been here two weeks and you're just getting around
to visit me.

HARRY

I'm not a free man, Jim. I've got things to do.

153

JIM

More important things, of course.

HARRY

I'm sorry, Jim. I just couldn't. . . .

JIM

Yeah—(*Bitterly*) Well, how do you like the place?

HARRY

How long will they keep you here?

JIM

I don't know.

HARRY

I was wondering if I could visit with your doctor a few minutes. . . .

JIM

What for?

HARRY

Just to talk to him. Do you suppose he's in?

JIM

The office is down the hall, on your right. Ask for Dr. Bellman.

HARRY
(*To* ANN)

Excuse me.

(*He goes off.*)

154

ANN

Why were you so mean to Harry?

JIM

You'd think he'd take a little more interest in his brother.

ANN

Some of your students called. They heard you were sick.

JIM

How did they know to call you?

ANN
(*Hesitantly*)

I had your phone disconnected and the calls switched to me.

JIM

Well, that's fine. I'll only have to connect it again, that's all.

ANN

The company would have taken it out anyway. There was no one to pay the bill. You can't go back to that cold-water flat, Jim. The doctors say it would be too depressing.

JIM

They didn't say that to me.

ANN

Dr. Bellman—Dr. Schlesinger—they all said it.

JIM

To you?

ANN

Yes.

JIM

It's nice of them to be so concerned. Are they going to find me an apartment?

ANN

We'll manage, dear. Don't worry.

JIM

I see. (*A pause*) Do my students know what happened?

ANN

No. I wasn't sure what to tell them. They all want to visit you. I had quite a time putting them off. I said you were in the hospital for tests. It's vague enough. They say what kind of tests, and I tell them I really don't know.

JIM

They must think it's awfully mysterious. Well, I'll reach them when I get out.

ANN

Jim—I—I had to tell them not to wait for you—to go ahead and find another teacher.

JIM
(*Turns on her quickly. His tone is sharp*)
Why?

ANN

I had to, Jim. Dr. Bellman said it might be some time. I had to say there was no way of knowing how long you'd be sick, and it was better not to wait.

JIM
(*Looks at her briefly*)

I see.

ANN
(*An attempt at brightness*)
Everyone's been calling about you.

JIM

That's great. Did you reach Davidson and Walker?

ANN

I called them, Jim—really, I did. Dr. Walker said he couldn't take the responsibility. And you know how Davidson feels.

JIM
(*Disillusioned and angry*)
I see. Well, it seems that the people I counted on to say I'm well are the very ones who now say I'm sick.

ANN

Why do you say that?

JIM

I'm still here. That's why I say it.

ANN

We're doing everything we can. . . .

JIM

I know, Ann, I know. I know, I know. . . . (HARRY *comes back to table.* JIM *turns to him*) What did he say?

HARRY

I only spoke to him for a minute.

JIM

So?

HARRY
(*Disturbed*)

Apparently, Jim, you've said and done things since you've been here that give them the right to have doubts about you.

JIM

What did I say?

HARRY

I don't know—he wouldn't tell me, of course, but . . .

ANN

Dr. Bellman did tell me you showed a great deal of antagonism and resentment. . . .

JIM

What do they expect, for God's sake? They probe and pry and get you upset—and then expect you to behave like a normal human being.

HARRY

They're the bosses here, Jim.

JIM

But they don't even tell me what I'm here for.

ANN

You should try to co-operate, dear. Dr. Bellman said there were many questions you refused to answer.

JIM

It's none of their business.

ANN

But it is, Jim. They only want to help you. You should tell them everything.

JIM

Do you know they think I'm a potential murderer?

ANN

That's ridiculous, Jim.

JIM

The attendant told me.

ANN

And you listened to him?

JIM

It's logical, isn't it? They feel I've turned my hostility against myself.

159

HARRY

Jim, listen to *me*.

ANN

Tell them everything, Jim, and tell them the truth.

JIM

But I have—I haven't lied about a thing. Everything I said—to Schlesinger—to Bellman—to the nurses—to the psychologist who gave me the Rorschach test—to anyone here—has been the truth.

HARRY

Ann, may I speak to Jim alone, please?

ANN

(*Apprehensive*)

What can you have to say that I mustn't hear?

HARRY

Ann, after all, what's wrong with wanting to speak to my brother?

ANN

Why am I in the way?

HARRY

Ann, it's nearly two o'clock. People will be coming in. Give me a few minutes with Jim alone.

ANN

Where can I go? I'm not allowed anywhere but here.

160

JIM

Go to the office—ask one of the nurses—go out for coffee
—anything. Ann, don't start crying. (ANN, *wiping her eyes,
rises and goes off*) I can't stand those tears. (*Turns away,
irritably*) Well, go ahead and talk. What did you want to
tell me?

HARRY

First, you've got to stop shooting off your mouth. Now
listen to me for a change. I've got something I want to tell
you. From the minute I learned you were in this place, I've
been worried. Back home I asked around quietly—a doctor
friend, a lawyer friend—I had to be careful. You know what
Keysport is like. If it got out I had a brother in an . . .

JIM

Insane asylum.

HARRY
(*Apologizing*)

Well, you know, Jim, it sounds awful. There's Helen and
the children—and it just isn't good for my business.

JIM

So?

HARRY

They couldn't advise me, Jim. They said the law in this
state may be different from ours. But they gave me the names
of a couple of people to see. . . .

JIM

Did you talk to them?

HARRY

Yes, this morning.

JIM

And?

HARRY

They can't do a thing. You're in the hands of the authorities now. The police picked you up and a city hospital has you in custody. If you want to get out of here, you've got to play ball.

JIM

How?

HARRY

In two ways. First, as far as the hospital is concerned. (*He looks around*) You know how to handle a cop, don't you?

JIM

How do you mean?

HARRY

Jim, I have never paid a fine in my life. Because I know that I never know more than a cop. He's the smart one—not me. And it's "Yes, officer" and "No, officer" and "I'm sorry, sir." Don't try to know more than these people. If you want to get out of here, you'll have to swallow everything. (JIM *makes a gesture of protest*) Well, what's so tough about that, you proud son of a bitch? Don't I have to do it every day of my life? I've got a lousy insurance business, so I get drunk

162

with a client, watch him make passes at Helen—and flatter the hell out of him. Do you think I like it? (JIM *looks at him*) It's no different in here. It's no different out there. Try it. What can you lose?

JIM

A model patient?

HARRY

Try it.

JIM
(*After a pause, quietly*)
What else?

HARRY

With Ann it will be harder. I don't know how things were with you in the past few years. You seldom wrote. But you were separated. Is that right?

JIM

Yes.

HARRY

I went down to that address you gave me in the letter. Your apartment's been rented to somebody else.

JIM
(*Stunned*)
And all my things?

163

HARRY

Everything's been moved back to Ann's place. The landlady told me.

JIM

She's got rid of my students. I have no place to go. . . .

HARRY

She's made you completely dependent on her, Jim. That's what she set out to do, and that's what she's achieved.

JIM

Why, for God's sake? What does she want of me?

HARRY

She loves you, Jim. She wants you back. She told the doctor that. I won't try to explain it. I think there's something distorted in taking advantage of your being here to get you back this way. But I don't question that she loves you—and my advice to you is to be in love with her. That's the only way you'll get out of here quickly.

JIM
(*Quickly*)

I can't do it, Harry.

HARRY

You lived with her for nine years. It can't be that difficult.

JIM

You don't know.

164

HARRY

Ann is the only one who can help you, Jim.

JIM

I can't keep walking out on myself like that.

HARRY

Well, any other way will mean months—not in this place, because they can't keep you here. There's some kind of law, I was told, about a city hospital. You can be sent away to a state hospital, if that's what she wants.

JIM

Harry, I'm afraid of this place. When I think of an insane asylum ...

HARRY

State hospital.

JIM

State hospital, I know. Forgive me, I don't care for the euphemism.

HARRY

Is there a euphemism for your life with Ann? (JIM *looks at* HARRY) That's the choice—the only choice.

JIM
(*Long pause*)
I don't know if she'll believe me now.

HARRY

She wants to believe you.

JIM

God—just to get out of here, I'd . . .

HARRY

Now, don't get any notions that'll make trouble for you. You won't be a free man when you get out. You'll be released in her custody—that's one thing.

JIM

But after a while—when I'm out . . .

HARRY

There's no "after a while" for you, Jim. You're trapped. I won't be able to help you, Jim—no one will. It's a terrible thing to say, but no one can walk into that record office and make your name disappear. That's how it is. . . . People on the outside are more scared of someone who's been in a mental hospital than they are of one who's been to jail. You'll not only be living with Ann, you'll be living with the fear of exposure. It's a tough decision to make, Jim. Telling the truth has gotten you nowhere. You're going to have to play ball— tell them the things they want to hear. (*He suddenly feels guilty and he kicks an imaginary piece of paper with his foot*) I know it goes against the grain. Certainly—no man is better for selling himself, believe me—and you're likely to suffer more than most. (*He looks at his brother*) Jim—you want to get out!

(JIM *nods his head slowly.*)

(*The lights fade quickly.*)

ACT THREE

SCENE II

The same.
Four days later—Monday.
DR. BELLMAN, DR. BARROW, MISS WINGATE *and* GREGORY
are standing near a table.

MISS WINGATE

Last Friday he played some ping pong.

GREGORY

That was the first time since he came to "one."

DR. BARROW

Was this voluntary or did he have to be urged?

MISS WINGATE

He asked someone to play with him, as I remember.

(*She looks at* GREGORY.)

GREGORY

That's right.

DR. BARROW
(*Looks at* BELLMAN. *Then, to* GREGORY)
Has he been eating?

GREGORY

Much better, the last few days.

MISS WINGATE

And Saturday he went to the movie we had in the auditorium.

DR. BELLMAN

Would you say he's adjusted to hospital routine?

GREGORY

I think so.

DR. BELLMAN

Does he speak of his wife?

GREGORY

Yes—some.

DR. BELLMAN

Would you get him for me, Mr. Gregory?

(GREGORY *leaves right.*)

MISS WINGATE

Mr. Downs reads a great deal. I thought of asking him to prepare a quiz show. The men get pretty tired of the games we have here.

DR. BARROW
(*Looks at* BELLMAN)

I know.

DR. BELLMAN

There isn't anything we can do.

168

MISS WINGATE

Would you approve of the quiz-show idea?

DR. BELLMAN

We'll think about it, Miss Wingate.

(JIM *enters.*)

MISS WINGATE

Yes, Doctor.

DR. BARROW

Hello, Jim. May we see you please?

DR. BELLMAN
(*Turns*)

Hello, Mr. Downs.

(MISS WINGATE *exits.*)

DR. BARROW

How do you like it down here?

JIM
(*Tentatively*)

All right.

DR. BARROW

You look much better than you did upstairs.

JIM

I was in quite a state up there, I guess.

DR. BARROW

I would say so, Jim. Shall we sit down? (*They go to a table.* DR. BELLMAN *stands behind* JIM. DR. BARROW *looks at* DR. BELLMAN, *arranges her papers*) You won't mind if we give you a little test.

JIM
(*Frightened*)

Not at all.

(*He turns to look at* DR. BELLMAN, *who is standing impassively.*)

DR. BARROW

This is a word-association test. I will give you a word from this list and I want you to answer with the first word that comes into your mind. For example, if I say "apple"—you may say "fruit" or "red" or "orange" or anything that occurs to you, but don't take time to think about it. The first word that occurs to you—remember. (*She sets her stop watch*) All right. Black.

JIM

White.

(DR. BARROW *notes the word and the time taken.*)

DR. BARROW

Street.

JIM

Car.

DR. BARROW

Suicide.

JIM
(*A momentary catch*)

Death.

DR. BARROW

Bed.

JIM

Soft.

DR. BARROW

Friend.

JIM

Good.

DR. BARROW

Trouble.

JIM
(*A brief pause. He repeats the word*)

Trouble—trouble.

DR. BARROW

Are you repeating the word?

JIM

I guess so. Trouble is trouble. I can't think of anything else.

DR. BARROW

All right. Mother.

JIM

Father.

DR. BARROW

Murder.

JIM

Bad.

DR. BARROW

Marriage.

JIM

Love.

DR. BARROW

Wife. (JIM *looks at* BARROW *briefly—he is wrestling with himself. She repeats the word*) Wife.

JIM
(*Quietly*)

Sweetheart.

DR. BELLMAN
(*Severely*)

Just a minute, Mr. Downs. Dr. Barrow asked you to respond immediately, didn't she?

JIM

Yes—I . . .

DR. BELLMAN

In her instructions she said, "Don't take time to think of an answer. We want the first word that occurs to you." Isn't that right?

JIM

Yes.

DR. BELLMAN

In the light of what we know about your relationship with your wife, would you say that "sweetheart" represented an instinctive response?

JIM

Well . . .

DR. BARROW

We are trying to help you, Jim. You don't have to lie to us.

JIM

I'm not lying—I . . .

DR. BELLMAN

There must have been some reason for your answer. You are obviously trying to mislead us.

JIM

No—I'm not. Why should I?

DR. BELLMAN

If Dr. Barrow had said "Charlotte," we might have expected such an answer.

JIM
(*Fighting for his life*)
No, Doctor—honestly. That isn't true any more.

DR. BELLMAN
Can you really tell what is true at this point?

JIM
I think so—I . . .

DR. BELLMAN
Either you were lying before—or you are lying now.

DR. BARROW
(*Sympathetically*)
The discrepancy is too obvious, Jim. You can see that.

JIM
(*Forcefully*)
Isn't it *possible* to realize I've made a mistake?

DR. BELLMAN
But this represents . . .

Together

DR. BARROW
Of course it's possible.

JIM
(*Desperately*)
I was in love with my wife when I married her.

174

DR. BARROW
You don't have to defend yourself, Jim. We are not asking you to be in love with her, if your feelings have . . .

JIM
(*Protesting*)
But I am—I am—I *am* in love with her. . . .

DR. BELLMAN
And the quarrels and bickering . . .

JIM
That happens to anybody. I lived with her, didn't I? We had years together. . . .

DR. BELLMAN
The things you told Dr. Schlesinger . . .

JIM
I was bitter. I was resentful. I had taken my life. . . . I was mad at everybody. I must have said the things that gave only one side of the picture.

DR. BELLMAN
You realize this change is rather sudden.

JIM
(*Now he is angry*)
I don't know about that. I don't know what constitutes a

sudden change. But I've been in the hospital more than two weeks, and I've had time to think. I've been away from both Ann—*and* Charlotte—and I have a perspective I didn't have before.

DR. BELLMAN

And what do you think now?

JIM

I think of the good things I had with Ann. When we were living together I—I—I must have magnified the irritations and—made them important.

DR. BELLMAN

And Charlotte?

JIM
(*A pause*)

I—I indulged myself, I guess—I . . .

(*He stops.*)

DR. BELLMAN
(*A pause*)

What were you going to say?

JIM

I was going to say that most men do, at some time or other, but I realize that I have no right to say that.

DR. BELLMAN

Why?

JIM

Because I don't know, for one thing. And even if it were true, that's no excuse for me.

DR. BELLMAN

I see. (*A pause*) Do you want to go on with the test, Dr. Barrow?

DR. BARROW

I think that's enough for now.

DR. BELLMAN

All right, Mr. Downs, you may go.

(JIM *gets up silently and leaves.*)

DR. BARROW

(DR. BARROW *waits until* JIM *has gone, looks at* BELLMAN—*then, slowly*)

I am inclined to believe him.

DR. BELLMAN

We'll wait and see. Let's check the test.

(*He sits at the table.*)

(*The lights fade quickly.*)

177

ACT THREE

Scene III

The same.

Three days later—Thursday. Visiting day.

Some visitors have already arrived and are sitting with the patients at the tables. All the patients expecting visitors are standing in the corridor in a group at the right. Even patients not expecting anyone are in the group, getting a vicarious joy out of seeing others embrace and laugh and cry. MR. CARLISLE *is one of these.*

JIM *looks anxiously at the door. The bell rings. An attendant unlocks the door and the visitor enters. If the visitor has a package, and he usually has, the contents are examined at the door. When approved, the attendant turns to the group and calls out the name of the patient being visited.* ANKORITIS *is being visited by his wife. They are already at a table.* MAJOR's *sister is talking and laughing with him at another table.*

When the lights come up, ANN *and her brother,* TOM, *have already been admitted.*

GREGORY
(*Examining* ANN's *package, looks at* TOM *and then calls*)

Downs.

179

JIM

(*Meets them at center table*)

Ann! I've been waiting. (*Shakes hands with* TOM) Hello, Tom. It's nice of you to come.

TOM

(*Tall, heavy-set—smiles as he takes* JIM's *hand*)

You look fine, Jim.

JIM

I feel wonderful—better than in months.

ANN

Dr. Bellman was telling me this morning that you'd improved a great deal.

JIM

Let's sit down. (*They go to a table where* MAJOR *is sitting*) What did you bring, Ann?

ANN

(*Gives him the bag*)

Some fruit—candy.

JIM

(*To* TOM)

You have no idea what her being here every visiting day has meant to me. (ANN *smiles. They sit down,* JIM *right of the table—*ANN *to the left.* TOM *takes a chair from in front of the table and sits to the left of* ANN) She's been wonderful, Tom—simply wonderful. The whole hospital knows about her.

ANN
(*Laughing*)

Oh, Jim ...

JIM

It's true. Down here ... (*He turns to the group*) You see those fellows standing over there? Well, sometimes they just stand there—even though no one ever comes to see them. I suppose, vicariously, they are visiting with everyone who comes in. After I leave you, Ann, each time one or another of them has come to me and said, you have a fine wife—I can tell. (ANN *laughs*) Seriously.

ANN

Thank you, Jim. It's very nice of you to say that.

JIM

Ann—we've wasted a lot of time on misunderstandings....

ANN

Yes, Jim.

JIM

We'll make it up, Ann—you'll see.

ANN

If only I could believe you, Jim. This is the first time since you've been in the hospital you've spoken like this.

JIM

Ann, I ...

ANN

You were so impatient with me. Of course I realize what you were going through.

JIM

I'm sorry, Ann. It took time. Even after I got down here, I wasn't over the drug yet. I said a lot of things I really didn't mean—and I'm sorry. Ann, we're in love—we've always been in love. You know that.

ANN

I know I've always loved you, Jim.

JIM

I know.

ANN

Jim . . .

JIM

Wait, let me finish. Being here was quite a shock—the whole experience is a shock. I've had time for lots of thinking, and one thing's become clear to me. I have a different sense of values from what I had before. For one thing, I don't have the unrealistic ambitions I had before. If I can settle down to a good job, that's all I want.

ANN

But . . .

JIM

I know what you're thinking. Look, Ann, if I have to, I'd even give up the theatre.

ANN

Let's hope you don't have to do that.

JIM

But I would.

ANN

You do mean this, Jim, don't you?

JIM

Yes, I do.

ANN
(*Pause*)
I had a long talk with Dr. Bellman this morning. . . .

JIM

What'd he say?

ANN

He's been getting fine reports about you. He said it may only be a few more days now.

JIM

He did?

183

ANN

Now you mustn't get impatient. But he did say you were better.

TOM

Since it may only be a few days before you're discharged . . .

ANN

Tom, really, I . . .

TOM

Now let me take care of this, Ann. Ann didn't want me to come along, but I insisted. Now I don't want you to feel that, because I'm Ann's brother I'm taking her side. I like you, Jim—I always have, and that's got nothing to do with Ann.

JIM
(*Apprehensive*)

What is it, Tom?

TOM

Well, now wait—I'll get to it. I just want to say that Ann didn't get her big brother to come down here to—eh—put a whip to you—you know what I mean—eh—so eh—well, what it is—is just that Ann's friends and her doctor don't think it would be smart for Ann to take you back.

JIM
(*In desperate panic. He can hardly speak*)

Why not?

TOM

After all, you left her—you've been carrying on with another girl—you even tried to reach her here in the hospital.

JIM

But that's all over. I don't want to see this girl again.

TOM

Well, that's what we want to find out, Jim. If you're on the level about not wanting to see this girl again, then I think you ought to write her a letter and say so very plainly.

JIM

All right.

TOM

Or—if you prefer—if you want to see this girl and tell her how you feel—then I'll go with you.

JIM
(*In a trap*)

Sure.

TOM

Ann has taken a terrible beating, Jim. All her friends—and, I must say, I agree with them—feel that she mustn't be hurt again. So—now that you may be getting out, this is what I want to say. You don't have to feel any obligation to Ann because of what she did for you in the hospital. Ann would have done that anyway, because she loves you. And you don't have to say now what you want to do—there's no pressure—no obligation. If you want to think about it—take your time. Only, once you give your word—that has to be it.

JIM

Of course.

ANN
(*To* JIM)

Please think it over, darling. I don't want you to make a mistake.

JIM

I know, dear. I—think it's very fair of Tom to put it this way.

TOM

You're a free man, Jim.

JIM

Hm-hmmmm.

TOM

Now take your time. . . .

JIM

Ann—what can I say? (*He can hardly breathe*) I—I know we're in love. You, certainly, have been more decent than I deserve. . . .

ANN

Not at all, dear.

JIM

I said I was finished with—with Charlotte. I meant it. If— you'll have me back—I want to go back. I'm sure things will be better between us than they were.

ANN

They will, darling. I know they will.

JIM

I've been through quite an experience, Ann. You know that better than anyone. I'm not over it yet—and—I'm still in this place. You'll have to give me time, Ann. After all, I—I've been reclaimed, so to speak.

ANN

It's been difficult, I know.

(DR. BELLMAN *enters.*)

DR. BELLMAN

Hello, Mrs. Downs.

ANN

How do you do, Dr. Bellman?

(DR. BELLMAN *goes to* ANKORITIS *and speaks with him and his wife.*)

JIM

I'm tired, Ann. Will you forgive me?

ANN

Certainly.

187

TOM

And we'll take care of that other matter when you get out.

JIM

Sure. It was good to see you, Tom. (*To* ANN) 'Bye, darling.

> (*He smiles, not sure whether to embrace her or not. He takes a step to her—she, to him. Slowly, their arms go out and they embrace. Then he turns, and walks slowly off.*)

CARLISLE

She never misses coming to see you on a visiting day.

ANN
> (*Has watched* JIM *go off, then turns to* TOM)

Wait for me. I want to speak to Bellman a minute. (*She crosses to* BELLMAN) Dr. Bellman?

DR. BELLMAN
> (*Talking with* ANKORITIS)

Excuse me. (*He steps over to* ANN *and smiles brightly*) How are you, Mrs. Downs?

ANN

I'm fine, thank you, Doctor. I agree with you. There's a tremendous improvement in Jim.

DR. BELLMAN

Do you think he's telling the truth now?

ANN

I'm sure of it.

DR. BELLMAN

Well, we'll see. How do you feel about taking him back?

ANN

I love him, Doctor.

DR. BELLMAN

And this other girl?

ANN

That's finished.

DR. BELLMAN

I'll have another talk with him myself tomorrow. It may only be another day.

ANN

Thank you, Doctor.

(ANN *goes to* TOM. *He helps her on with her coat.*)

(*The lights fade quickly.*)

ACT THREE

SCENE IV

The same.

The next day—Friday.

DR. BELLMAN *and* JIM *are seated at a table.* BELLMAN, *left—*JIM, *right.*

The interview is already in progress.

DR. BELLMAN

Then you think you feel differently now from when you came here?

JIM

Yes, I do.

DR. BELLMAN

In what way do you feel differently?

JIM

I suppose in the matter of learning about myself. I don't think I have the unrealistic ambitions I had before.

DR. BELLMAN

What do you mean by that?

191

JIM

Well, after a certain number of years in a profession without making the grade, I'd say it was realistic to think in terms of other work.

DR. BELLMAN

What do you plan to do if you leave here?

JIM

Go home.

DR. BELLMAN

Is that all?

JIM

Well—I'd need time to recover....

DR. BELLMAN

Recover from what?

JIM

From this whole experience.

DR. BELLMAN

Then you don't really think you're well yet.

JIM

Yes, I do....

DR. BELLMAN

Then why did you say "recover"?

JIM

I meant . . .

DR. BELLMAN

What?

JIM

Well, I have no job. It will take time to find something.

DR. BELLMAN

Recover doesn't mean finding a job.

JIM

I know that. I simply used the word to . . .

DR. BELLMAN

How?

JIM

In the sense of getting back to normal.

DR. BELLMAN

And what do you mean by normal?

JIM

Well, living here is . . .

DR. BELLMAN

Yes?

JIM

(*A pause—catching himself*)

By normal I only meant working again—living at home—being back with my wife.

DR. BELLMAN

Then you don't really have a plan for your future.

JIM

Well, I could start by going back to my teaching.

DR. BELLMAN

Are you a good teacher?

JIM

I think so.

DR. BELLMAN

Can you make a living by your teaching?

JIM

Fair.

DR. BELLMAN

Enough to support you and your wife?

JIM

If we're careful. I'll have to find more regular work, of course.

DR. BELLMAN

What kind of work?

JIM

I don't know at the moment, Doctor. I—I'm not unintelligent—I'm sure there's something I can do.

DR. BELLMAN

I see. Do you feel you will need psychiatric help when you leave here?

JIM

Do you think I will?

DR. BELLMAN

I'm asking you.

JIM

I just don't know, Doctor.

DR. BELLMAN

Do you feel you're cured?

JIM

I think so.

DR. BELLMAN

Then you don't think you will need help on the outside.

JIM

No. I don't.

DR. BELLMAN

One more thing. Do you feel that having been here will affect your future?

JIM

How do you mean?

DR. BELLMAN

How would you react if the people you worked with knew you had been in a mental hospital?

JIM

If they know—they know. There's nothing I can do about it.

DR. BELLMAN

But how would you feel?

JIM

I'd expect them to think of me in the light of the present. If my work is satisfactory I can only hope the past will play no part in their judgment.

DR. BELLMAN

I see. And you feel now you're ready to go home.

JIM

Yes.

DR. BELLMAN

When do you think you should leave?

JIM

That's up to you, Doctor.

THE SHRIKE

DR. BELLMAN
(*A brief pause*)
That's all for now.

JIM
(*Gets up, starts off, turns*)
Is it unreasonable to ask how long it will be?

DR. BELLMAN
(*Slowly*)
No.

JIM
(*His throat is dry*)
Then may I know?

DR. BELLMAN
(*Looks at* JIM— *a long* "Hmmmmm")
Call your wife.

JIM
(*Unable to believe*)
What?

DR. BELLMAN
Call your wife. You may go home today.

JIM
(*Simply*)
Thank you, Doctor. (*A few steps back*) May I call from here?

DR. BELLMAN

Yes.

JIM

Thank you.

DR. BELLMAN

You may use that phone.

> (*Indicates phone on table.* JIM *goes to the phone.*
> DR. BELLMAN *rises—to* JIM) You'll be in her custody,
> you understand.

JIM

> (*Nods.* DR. BELLMAN *leaves*)

Yes.

> (*He dials a number, and waits. The lights fade on
> all but* JIM) Ann? I'm discharged. I can leave today.
> Dr. Bellman just said so. Ann, would you bring a
> tie and my overcoat? Thank you, dear. You won't be
> long—will you? (*He hangs up. The tears have started.
> He knows he is trapped. He turns and slowly walks
> across the stage, convulsed with sobs.*)

> (*Curtain*)